What the E

"Angela & Steve's perpetu
heights through the arts a
venting themselves, sums up who they are. Robert is the icing and cherry on top! His deep soul and vast spirit resonate through all that he declares throughout the book. This book is a reflection of these generous, knowledgeable and well-rounded entrepreneurs who wish to share their wisdom by encouraging and teaching others. You will finish reading this guide feeling uplifted and ready to soar!"

Simone DePaolo. Entertainer, Choreographer and Teacher

"A book truly built from the heart, soul & mind. Angela, Steve & Robert bring their infinite wisdom & eclectic insight to the reader through years of multi-dimensional experience & passion for their craft. They transform the science of successful business ownership into an art form while inspiring dance teachers that with self-motivation & wherewithal one's goals are never far from reach. An essential library staple for beginners or the most seasoned of veterans!"

Jessica Rizzo, MA Dance Education PK-12/Higher Education and Choreographer

"I have known Steve and Angie for over 10 years. I have worked with them at teaching colleges and have seen the success of their studio and business. They have a superior work ethic and have dedicated their lives to bringing cutting edge, progressive thinking and clear straight forward methods of running a studio and teaching dance. Together with Robert, who is an inspiring motivational speaker, I cannot think of three people with a more positive outlook on life and this most definitely spills over into their businesses."

Dolly Kelepecz, Full-time Lecturer, University of Nevada at Las Vegas. Owner of D.K. BodyBalancing Method

"Steve and Angela are dedicated, creative dance teachers, studio owners and entrepreneurs who have seen such success in the industry. Don't you want to know their secret? Take a moment to glean inspiration and wisdom from these two powerhouses, together with the proven techniques and practical advice of esteemed motivator Robert Landau."

Deborah Searle, Founder, Dance Informa Magazine

It's Your Turn!

The Success Blueprint for the Dance Teacher

by

Steve Sirico, Angela D'Valda Sirico and Robert Landau

The Dance Teacher Web Advisor Series

Published by DanceTeacherWeb.com, LLC

Printed in the United States of America

Library of Congress Cataloging-in-Publication Data
Sirico, Steve, D'Valda Sirico, Angela, Landau, Robert
It's Your Turn! The Success Blueprint for the Dance School Teacher

ISBN 978-0-9856910-3-5

Contents

Who We Are

Steve Sirico

ORIGINALLY from Norwalk, Connecticut, Steve excelled in track and football. He attended the University of Tennessee at Martin on a sports scholarship. Deciding to switch and make his career in the world of dance, he studied initially with Mikki Williams and then in New York with Charles Kelley and Frank Hatchett. He appeared in a number of theatre productions such as *Damn Yankees, Guys and Dolls* and *Mame* in New York and around the country, and in industrials and television shows. He was contracted to appear as the lead dancer in the Valerie Peters Special, a television show filmed in Tampa, Florida. After meeting Angela D'Valda during the filming, they formed the Adagio act of D'Valda & Sirico coached by Bob DeVoye and Fred Favorite. Together, they appeared in theatres, clubs and on such television shows as David Letterman, Star Search and the Jerry Lewis Telethon.

In 1982, they were contracted to Europe, and appeared in a variety of shows in Spain, Portugal, Sweden, Finland, Switzerland and Italy. They then left for London, England, where they appeared as Guest Artists for Wayne Sleep (formerly of the Royal Ballet) in his show *Dash* at the Dominion Theatre.

Steve and Angela have owned and directed their dance studio in Fairfield, Connecticut, for the past twenty-six years. Steve is author of his Jazz Dance syllabus and co-author of a Partner syllabus—both of which have been used for teacher training by Dance Educators of America. He continues to adjudicate and teach for major dance organizations.

He recently has taught at the Interdanz Conference in San José, Costa

Rica, as well as at The International Dance Teachers Conference at London's Royal Ballet School. He choreographs for theatres, television and conventions, and D'Valda & Sirico recently choreographed the opening to the National Speaker's Association convention held at New York City's Marriott Marquis on Broadway.

Steve is President and Co-Founder of the website Dance Teacher Web, designed as the ultimate online resource and training tool for dance teachers and dance school owners worldwide. The website features hundreds of videos and articles presented by a renowned team of master teacher and coaches. Dance Teacher Web produces a yearly conference in Las Vegas where hundreds of teachers learn from the top master teachers and business professionals in an intimate setting unlike any other dance teacher event. The Dance Teacher Web Live event is held in the summer. For more information visit www.danceteacherweb.com or www.danceteacherexpo.com You can connect with Steve at steve@danceteacherweb.com

Angela D'Valda Sirico

ORIGINALLY from England, Angela spent her early years in Hong Kong where she studied with Carol Bateman. She continued her training at Arts Educational Trust in England. Upon moving to New York City, New York, she studied with Martha Graham and Matt Mattox, before appearing with the Matt Mattox Company. Angela toured with the first *Disney On Parade* show, working with Disney and NBC. Contracted to the Teatro Nacional of Buenos Aires, she performed for one year and spent an additional year as a featured soloist at the Teatro Maipo, Argentina. Traveling to Madrid, Spain, she danced for Spanish television in a weekly variety show, *Tarde Para Todos,* and from there decided to form her own dance company. With the company, she choreographed and performed in theatres and on television throughout Spain.

Angela met her husband, Steve, while they worked together on a television special, *The Valerie Peters Show,* filmed in Tampa, Florida. In 1979, they formed the Adagio act D'Valda & Sirico coached by Bob DeVoye and Fred Favorite, appearing in theatres, clubs and on such television shows as *David Letterman, Star Search* and the *Jerry Lewis Telethon.* In 1982, they were contracted to Europe and appeared in a variety of shows in Spain, Portugal, Sweden, Finland, Switzerland and Italy. They then left for London, England, where they appeared as Guest Artists for Wayne Sleep (formerly of the Royal Ballet) in his show *Dash* at the Dominion Theatre.

Angela and Steve have owned and directed their dance studio in Fairfield, Connecticut, for the past twenty-six years. Angela served as chairperson for the Tri State panel of the Royal Academy of Dance and is author of a Lyrical Jazz syllabus and co-author of a Partner syllabus currently used by teachers worldwide. She continues to adjudicate and teach for major dance organizations, and choreographs for theatre, television and conventions. She was commissioned by Boston Ballet II to choreograph the highly acclaimed *Brother Can You Spare A Dime?* D'Valda & Sirico recently choreographed the opening to the National Speaker's Association convention held at New York City's Marriott Marquis on Broadway. She is also a regular faculty member at the International Dance Teachers Conference, hosted at London's Royal Ballet School.

Angela is the President and Co-Founder of the website, Dance Teacher Web, which has become the trusted online resource and training tool for dance teachers and dance-school owners worldwide. Dance Teacher Web produces a yearly conference in Las Vegas where hundreds of teachers learn from the top master teachers and business coaches in an intimate setting unlike any other dance teacher event. The Dance Teacher Web Live event is held in the summer. For more information visit: www.danceteacherweb.com or www.danceteacherexpo.com . You can connect with Angela at: angela@danceteacherweb.com

ROBERT LANDAU

ORIGINALLY from New York City, Robert comes from an artistic family. His father was a celebrated Symphony Orchestra Conductor (Maestro Siegfried Landau) and his mother was a modern dancer who studied with Martha Graham for many years. Rather than joining Martha's dance company, Irene Gabriel Landau formed her own. Upon retiring from dance, she became a professional photographer.

Robert Landau has delivered more than 2,100 presentations and workshops in more than twenty countries during his fifteen-year professional motivational-speaking career. Most of the year you will either find him speaking from the stage as a Keynote Speaker and/or as a seminar facilitator at numerous conferences. Robert also makes many appearances on radio and television broadcasts. One of his most recent appearances was on the world-wide HLN/CNN Cable News Networks. Landau is also an accomplished college and university motivational speaker. His best-selling online meditation course, *The 4 Minute Meditator System*, is available at www.The-4MinuteMeditator.com.

An accomplished actor in New York City, Robert was a celebrated international cruise director for ten years, visiting 300 ports of call on 400 cruises with major cruise lines. He is also the published author of the FUN Book Series, *How to Make Customer Service FUN!*, *How to Make Leadership FUN!* and *How to Make Communication FUN!* For more information visit: www.RobertLandauMotivation.com and www.The4MinuteMeditator.com You can connect with Robert at: rl@robertlandaumotivation.com

Acknowledgments

Steve and Angela

We would like to thank our families and friends—including our parents, siblings, aunts, uncles and cousins—for all of their support through the years. Steve would like to thank his dance teachers and mentors, Mikki Williams and Chuck Kelley, for pushing and believing in him. Angie would like to thank her teachers at Arts Educational Schools in London and Tring and Matt Mattox for amazing inspiration and guidance. Together, they want to give thanks to Fred Favorite and Bob DeVoye who coached and inspired them when they were putting their act together and gave them their first job as an adagio team. We are thrilled to have written this book with our good and longtime friend Robert Landau. It has been great to reconnect after many years, as he will always be like family. We could fill the pages of another entire book thanking all of the many wonderful people through the years who have come into our lives and have been instrumental in our success. You know who you are! A big "Thank You" to Dawn Macchiarelli our great friend who is our right *and* left hand and who is constantly there for us with her incredible insight and ideas. Asami Green has helped to make the book complete with her beautiful illustrations. We dedicate this book to all of the dance teachers we have worked with over the years. Here's to you and all that you do!

Robert

I would like to thank Geary for unending love and support. Heartfelt thanks also go out to Lynn Younger, Lynn Wallace and Sandra Abt for being true sisters and friends, and to my brother Peter, a sibling extraordinaire! Steve and Angie, you both are blessings beyond compare. Who could ask for better friends and creative partners? Working with you isn't work—it's pure joy! For that, I have Home Lines Cruises to thank, and Bramson Entertainment for having the unknown foresight to place us together on the same cruise ship so many moons ago. The stars were definitely in alignment! I would also like to thank Anne Kerven who, as editor of this book, was a dream to work with. And finally, Asami Green, the illustrations you've provided for this book are just what the doctor ordered.

Introduction

The Rehearsal—The Creative Blueprint

"Creativity makes a leap, then looks to see where it is."
–Mason Cooley

Think about it: A leap is something in dance that you throw yourself into, trusting that all will come out as planned in the end. The fine art of teaching dance implies that you take a leap each day you walk into your studio to facilitate a full day of classes. How will it all turn out? You won't know until you complete the task, just like a leap itself.

A leap isn't something that someone just suddenly gets up and does. You must be taught how to successfully execute a leap. In reality, it's a team effort between you, your teacher and the management of the studio or school that has created the opportunity in the first place. In the chapters that follow, we want you to consider us—Steve, Angela and Robert—as your "teaching team." Each of us has years of experience as teachers, both in and out of the dance industry. To teach is to inspire, to lead and to motivate. It's all about creating positive change and showing students how powerful they really are. We will stand by you and help you remember why you got into this profession in the first place—and how you can continue to do great things for years to come. This is our promise to you as you read through these pages.

Why would you need us by your side as part of your "teaching team"? We know all too well how demanding it is to be a dance teacher nowadays. Sometimes a teacher feels all alone, with little support or motivation to move forward on a daily basis. It is in the spirit of who you are and the wonderful work you do that we have created this book. Our wish is that by the time you finish reading it, you'll know that you have three partners in crime who stand by you and care enough to lift you to the next level of leadership, motivation and achievement as a teacher. Our goal is to get you to see things in a new light. We'll offer countless ideas that will serve as tools that you can put right into your teaching practice to effect true change. This change will benefit those you teach, as well as other staff, parents and the general public. If we can offer you at least two to three new ideas or perspectives, our goal in serving you will have been accomplished.

We've created this book using various themes that correspond to parts of your daily existence on the job. Each chapter features three different voices and opinions on the subject matter of the chapter. In each chapter's "Curtain Calls," you'll find a review of important and memorable points. A set of theatre curtains marks these all-important review pages so you can repeatedly refer to them long after you've finished reading the book. In other sections of the book, we suggest action plans and checklists that you can incorporate into your professional life today. Finally, we include a page for notes at the end of each chapter and a handy Reference Section at the end of the book.

It is with great joy and anticipation that we present this book to you. So take the leap with us and get ready to be inspired and motivated by what we'll be sharing with you. Acquiring new tools to help effect positive change in those who trust you as a mentor—that is what being a teacher is all about. Leap with us!

Chapter One

Back to Square One—Act One

Back to Square One—Act One: **Steve Sirico**

> "There are 3 types of people in this world: Those who make things happen, those who watch things happen and those who wonder what happened!"
>
> —*Mary Kay Ash*

Teachers are the lifeblood of the world. They are the doers and the ones who make things happen on many levels. Read that over and over again. Let's face it— teachers make this world go 'round. Don't think so? Think again! Every person on this planet has felt a teacher's impact. There is not one successful person who does not owe a big part of that success to a teacher. Conversely, bad teachers also have an effect, albeit negative. The point is that you are a special and powerful person, holding the keys that can impact the lives of your students, no matter what the student's age may be!

That is what I would like for you to place in your mind. Every teacher is important, and few are as crucial to your students as YOU! But before you focus on where you are today, let's go back to where you began. Remember, you were once a student, too. I think that this is one of the best parts of being a teacher—you never stop learning. Before you taught, you began at some point, just a rank beginner. Do you remember?

Let's journey back and think about the first time you taught. Then go back even further and think about your first dance lesson. WOW, I can remember my first dance course, a tap class that I was taking with my cousins. I don't really remember much about the content, but I do remember that I just loved to move to music. Being able to make sounds with my feet was incredible. I also remember my teacher as a kind and giving person who helped me develop my love of dance. After several years, I stopped taking dance lessons and became very involved in sports, which I still love very much to this day, especially football! But I was drawn back into dance, over and over again. In high school, I was the dancing man, the one everyone wanted to dance with. I was in my high school musical, taught the football team the latest dance moves and performed in Summer Theater. When I told my parents I was leaving college during my freshman year to pursue a career in dance, they supported me wholeheartedly. Lucky me! I dove in head first and have never looked back. It is true what they say: You don't choose dance—dance chooses you!

After two years of intense training I began to "sub" and assist in classes. My teacher, Mikki Williams, pushed me, believed in me and promoted me to everyone she knew. I had the honor of assisting Charles Kelley at various dance conventions, and loved working with teachers who were always so eager to learn and full of advice. Then I struck gold: I got my first job. It was an eight-week TV show in Florida, where the choreographer was none other than my future wife, Angela! After falling in love, we decided to put together our own act, one that would feature partner work with different styles of dance. We had the privilege of touring around the world for more than twelve years and taught master classes in more than twenty-five countries! One thing we noticed was that when we taught, it made us better dancers. We could hear the corrections that we were giving to others and that would reinforce our own corrections.

That is when it all started to click. We bought our studio and were ready for the next phase. But we still had a lot to learn about teaching and what it is to be a great teacher—especially when it came to teaching children. Through the years since then, I have learned a lot about many things, including myself! I am so grateful and honored to be part of a wonderful fraternity of dance teachers.

This chapter is about your beginning. It's about reflecting on where you have come from. From time to time, by going back, you can and will move forward. If you are at a plateau, going back can get you to the next phase.

OK, now it is your turn!

I would like for you to think about where you started and where you are today. Think about where you would like to go as a teacher. If you want to take the next step in your development as a dance teacher, it is important to reflect on where you have come from and harness all of the wonderful knowledge, life lessons and experience you have in your own personal tool chest. Sharing these important tools with yourself will keep you grounded and reset your all-important vision.

The key to moving forward is in your hands!

Where you are today and where you will be a year from now is all about your thought process and how you act upon those thoughts. Recall how you felt when you first started to teach—do you remember? If it has been awhile, think back. Think of your dreams, aspirations, goals and more! Now fast-forward to where you are today.

How has it worked out for you? If you are not where you want to be, you can change it—if you want to. You can improve it—if you want to. Believe me, I had plenty of setbacks. I could easily have retreated after the first setback, but I did not. If you persevere, you will keep finding new people who will help you along the way. Has that happened to you? If not, keep looking! Tell everyone you meet about your passion for teaching. The right people will be drawn to you. The right employers, fellow teachers and business opportunities will come your way—when you have your mind in the right place. Think not? Then don't be surprised when you get more of what you are already receiving!

Here are some BIG questions to ask yourself:

Do you believe in yourself as a dance teacher?

Are you the best you can be?

Are you frustrated and feel like you are stuck?

Are you happy with how you teach and what you are giving your students?

OK, if you do not have to make any big changes that is great. However, most of us have areas that we need to evaluate and analyze so that we can decide how to make the changes to improve our lives.

First, you need to have the right mindset. When you focus on all of the good things that you are creating, you will see the good and how to attract more of it into your life. Instead of focusing on the bad, focus on the excitement you felt when you first started teaching. The newness you savored, the uncertainty, the thrill of it all, and how your dreams and goals were right in front of you for the taking. If you have been teaching for awhile, you will want to block out the negativity that can so easily cloud your thoughts—if you haven't made that conscious effort already to guard against these thoughts. You must work at this. Try it for a month, then for two, then for six and then make it a lifetime habit.

Keep in mind that the thoughts you focus on will determine who you are! If you think about how this employer or student did you wrong, you may well become bitter. If you think about how horribly the studio owner treats you, you may grow disillusioned. On the other hand, if you think about how wonderfully lucky you are to be a teacher you will see all that is good. This keeps you in a good place mentally. Look, not everything will be perfect all the time. What is in life? After personally being a dance teacher for twenty-six years, I can tell you this: I remember the good—and not so good—times with gratitude for the lessons learned! Stay true to yourself, and you will attract what you seek.

Turning Your Dreams Into Reality

Everyone, at some point in his or her life, has dreamed of being somebody special, somebody big. Maybe you have fantasized about being the one who appears on Broadway, the prima ballerina or a sought-after choreographer. Or maybe you imagine yourself as one of the top dance teachers in the country or in demand worldwide. How many times have we dreamed of being rich, or successful, or happy with our relationships?

Often, we dream big dreams and have great aspirations. Unfortunately, our dreams remain just that—dreams—and our aspirations easily collect dust in our attics. This can be a sad turn of events in our lives. Instead of experiencing exciting adventures in self-actualization, we get caught up in the humdrum of day-to-day living, just barely existing.

But you know what? Life could be so much better if only we learn to aim higher and to act upon our goals. Set your goals high and then create an action plan on how to achieve those goals. Don't worry—in the coming chapters we will help you with ways to do this.

One big key to your success and growth will be how you handle the failures in your life, both personally and as a teacher. This just in: Being a teacher is hard work, despite what other people may think! We don't sit around all day just thinking creative thoughts and feeling great! It took Thomas Edison more than one thousand tries to get the light bulb right. Will you keep pushing through, even though times may get tough? In this book you will learn valuable lessons on how to achieve, how to set goals and reach them, and how to be all you can. You may even exceed your own expectations.

Here is something to think about: *Failure is the line of least persistence. Success occurs when opportunity meets preparation.*

Here is something sad to ponder on: *The average person will go to his grave with his music still in him.*

The best news of all is that you are reading this book and will gain knowledge and power to excel in all you do. Nothing can stop you, can you feel it?

> "Success is going from failure to failure without losing enthusiasm."
>
> —*Winston Churchill*

Bravo! Act One Curtain Calls

Remember these things:

- There is not one successful person who does not owe a big part of his or her success to a teacher
- You are a special and powerful person, with the keys and ability to impact the lives of your students
- You don't choose dance, dance chooses you!
- If you are at a plateau, going back can get you to the next phase
- If you want to take the next step in your development as a dance teacher, reflect on where you have come from
- Where you are today and where you will be a year from now is all about your thought process and how you act upon those thoughts
- If you persevere, you will keep finding new people that will help you along the way
- Focus on the good things that you are creating, and you will see the good and how to attract more of it into your life
- The thoughts you focus on will determine who you are!
- **Set your goals high and then create an action plan on how to achieve those goals**

Back to Square One—Act Two: **Robert Landau**

> "I am indebted to my father for living, but to my teacher for living well"
>
> —*Alexander the Great*

It seems as if life keeps getting more complicated as time moves on. This doesn't have to necessarily be a bad thing, but in today's crazy world of nonstop manic energy, it can be difficult to even hear oneself breathe. It seems as if we have less time to enjoy things because there's so much pressure to constantly produce. That's also what can happen with teaching. You can get so caught up in the day-to-day stress of getting the job done to the best of your ability, that the day is often over before you even get a chance to see how your classes went.

But what if the pressure to produce can be turned into a positive attribute that affects the outcome of doing a job well done? That's the great thing about teaching. You have the power to take things wherever you feel they should go. It's a positive spin on what it means to be in control. Pressure can be shifted from a negative into a positive and the applause you receive at the end of a class can prove that you invested your time and energy wisely.

The mind is a funny and powerful thing. We all too often give it permission to rule our lives and make all the important decisions for us. We believe everything it tells us without even thinking if it's bothering to connect with another important part of us, our heart. Your heart is where I'd like you to go right now.

Has teaching the process of dance been somewhat of a trying issue as of late? Are there times when you've felt pushed to the wall, emotionally exhausted and wondering how it is that you even made the decision to do what you do in this industry in the first place? Well pack your bags for a few minutes because I want to take you on a little journey. It's a journey into your past. Ready?

Our little excursion begins with a question; Can you remember the very first time you had the idea to teach dance?

See if you can remember that day, that moment, that feeling. This is bit of time from your past that you may recall or not. If you can't, that's just fine too. But if you can, see if you can formulate a sentence as to what it was that motivated you to become a dance teacher. Why did you want to do it? What did you hope to achieve by teaching dance?

Some may say, "I got into this because I wanted to share the sheer joy of dance with as many people as possible." Others might say, "My reason was to turn students on to something that's really creative and meaningful." Still others would say, "I wanted to effect change in young lives and give them something to hope for." Some might simply recall something more basic: "I wanted to earn a living doing something I love."

Whatever your reason might be—and here's where the heart comes in—I would think your reason for being a teacher has to do with your heart. How so? Could it be that teaching the fine art of dance has everything to do with your passion? When you teach, is there a past or future? Are you so totally into the moment that nothing else matters? Do the smiles of accomplishment on your students' faces mean the world to you? Is that a moment that you live for?

All of this and so much more could very well be the reasons you are where you are right here and now. There are no mistakes, there is no good or bad when it comes to fine art. It just "is." And so it is with you. Going back to square one helps get you back in touch with why you're in this crazy, nutso, but wonderful industry in the first place. Reconnecting with your original intent can help build more of a firm foundation so you can get to the next level with more ease with it comes to your future. It can also help you appreciate your present even more so than before.

I love to teach. Love may be a strong word, but it's exactly what I would use to describe what teaching is to me. It's not only a pleasure, it's an honor. Teaching is an art and a true gift, with an ability to work with students and help them grow. To me, teaching is just like performing. It brings a smile to my face, and if my face is smiling, I also know that my heart is smiling. All of this can be attributed to various thoughts and feelings that occur when I'm teaching. That in turn becomes a chemical reaction, and affects my health and my spirit in a positive and meaningful way. I could have had the worst day before I got to my class. But once I get up there and teach, I'm so in the moment that I'm all but invincible. Nothing negative matters. What I just heard on the news all but fades away, back into the vast darkness from which it came. There's no fear, there's no apprehension when I'm facilitating a class. None of the things that tend to hold me back from time to time in life are present when I'm in the process of teaching. If they are, I'm certainly not aware of them and that's exactly the point.

When I teach, life is a dream. I'm awake during it, consciously realizing how wonderful this dream really is. The level of energy is so great, I want to coast on it long after the class has ended. The feeling of still being revved up, hours after a class has ended, is the same feeling I experience hours after I've spoken to a large convention audience or performed onstage. Teaching is a fine art, and I'm proud to stand with those who do the same, each and every day, all over the world.

I often speak at events where, each month, a particular town or city awards a Teacher of the Month. This often gets me to thinking about teachers who made a difference in my life when I was a kid. The ones that immediately come to mind, whether they meant to or not, made such a huge difference in my life that I will never forget them. Their energy of love and support is forever etched in my heart, and I am more than thankful for what they did to help shape and mold me into the person I am today. And so it is with you. It may not be necessary to become The Teacher of the Decade, but know that in some of your students' hearts, that's what you already are and will always be. Now that's powerful! And it's all because you walked into your classroom and taught one fine day.

Our journey down life's path is nothing short of amazing. There are so many twists and turns that sometimes, it's all too easy to believe your mind when it tells you that today really stinks and you should get out of this industry altogether. When that happens, ask yourself if your heart is in agreement with this decision and then go back to why you decided to become a teacher in the first place. Do you still feel that way? Is there more to be done toward the wonderful work you do on a daily basis? If the answers to these questions are in the affirmative, then keep doing what you are doing and give yourself a huge pat on the back for the incredible, life-changing and meaningful work you do each and every day.

Leading and motivating students who want to learn a creative art changes lives, and can change the world as well. It all starts with one student and branches out from there. If people put down their guns and stopped rattling their sabers for a minute, and took a dance class, wouldn't the world be in a better place? The words and themes of harmony, teamwork, taking positive risks and achieving a measurable sense of accomplishment immediately come to mind. This is true everywhere and anywhere, from Singapore to Seattle.

When you have a bad day—and everyone does because it's a part of life—always remember how important you are to those who trust and depend on you to motivate them, to help them go beyond what they thought possible. You can unlock doors, remove emotional and psychological blocks, and create a positive vibe in people's lives. You may make more of a difference than you might ever know. A small ripple can end up creating the biggest wave.

Not everything is communicated at the time it is given. Students won't always tell you how much you mean to them. It's something that your heart knows. It's that really wonderful and warm feeling deep inside you that clues you in when you've done something that changed a life today. Changing lives for the better is what being a teacher is all about. You have the power to show people how to make things better for themselves and for those around them. You have the power to make people feel good about themselves. When the heart combines with the movement of the body and you add music to the mix, true magic occurs. It's healing magic. You are the conductor of that orchestra. Stand before your players, tall and proud. Keep on keeping on. There's a reason for what you do, and if you ever feel down and want to walk away from your calling as a teacher, go back to square one and listen to your heart. It remembers and knows the answers.

Bravo! Act Two Curtain Calls

Remember these things:

- You have the power to take things wherever you feel they should go
- Teaching the fine art of dance has everything to do with your passion
- When you teach there is no past or future, you are in the moment
- When you are in the moment, nothing else matters
- Teaching is an art and a true gift, an ability to work with students and help them grow
- Give yourself a huge pat on the back for to the incredible, life-changing and meaningful work you do each and every day
- Being a leader and a motivator for students changes lives and can change the world, as well
- The smallest ripple creates the biggest wave
- Changing lives for the better is what being a teacher is all about
- You have the power to make people feel good about themselves
- Your heart knows why you became a teacher. It always knows the answers

Back to Square One—Act Three: **Angela D'Valda Sirico**

> "To each there comes in their lifetime a special moment when they are figuratively tapped on the shoulder and offered the chance to do a special thing, unique to them and fitted to their talents. What a tragedy if that moment finds them unprepared or unqualified for that which could have been their finest hour."
>
> —*Winston Churchill*

You are a dance teacher, a member of a very honorable group and, every time you teach, you provide an amazing service to children and their parents. That might sound like a very grand statement, but you truly do teach the art of dance and also the art of life! So what made you become a teacher? Did you work as a professional dancer and then decide it was time to retire from performing? Did you get a degree in college, but felt you had more chance of teaching than performing? Did you graduate from high school and start to teach at the studio where you had studied for many years? Whatever the reason, you made that decision because, in one way or another, the whole idea was appealing to you. I can bet that one main reason was that you yourself loved to dance.

It is important to cast your mind back to when you first became a teacher, because that will reinforce to you the importance of continuing on. Your personal past will influence you greatly in the way you project yourself as a teacher to your employer, your students and their parents. A dance teacher in today's world has a constantly challenging role and one that can change almost year to year. Certainly in today's society, the way we teach and the way children learn is very different from that of even five years ago. So adaptability and willingness to keep your mind open to what is new and different goes a long way in your continued development as a teacher. Certainly, your experience directs the way that you think about and teach dance. But the ability to keep moving forward distinguishes you from the herd. Only by learning from our experiences can we understand how to move forward—and this really applies to any teacher, whether you are just starting out or have been doing it for years.

When I first started to teach I was only teaching professional dancers. Whenever Steve and I were in a show and in a place for any length of time, we would give classes to the most advanced dancers in any studio that would allow. It was fun. We would teach them our warm ups and our style—whether it was jazz, lyrical, partnering or ballet—and we were always well received because everyone knew we were featured in a show. It was great!

When Steve's former dance teacher wanted to sell her studio, we decided to buy it, thinking to ourselves that it would be easy! We had had plenty of experience teaching! Well, of course, we had a rude awakening. We soon found out that it is very different to teach children—it was a huge responsibility as we realized that we were teaching the art of dance and also the art of life. We went back to the drawing board and really evaluated how we would teach and with what syllabi. I had the good fortune of childhood training in the Royal Academy of Dance system. I went back to those roots, studied, took courses and re-memorized all the different levels, which let me teach my students that body of work. What a help that was, having a system to follow. I had also studied the Cecchetti and Vagonova styles wile growing up and found it helpful to incorporate parts of them into my more advanced classes. We found a syllabus for every style of dance, and those that we did not find, we created for ourselves. This helped us tremendously. It let us become better teachers and gave us a clearer measure of how our students were improving.

How hard it was to teach beginner classes! To find a way to be inspirational as a teacher to those students who have no coordination of the body and mind—that was difficult! It took me years to really find a system to help beginner students feel like dancers, with a lot of trial and error. Yet, the more I taught, the more I realized that I liked to teach. I found it immensely satisfying when I could see that I had actually helped my students to improve. It kept me going on days when I wondered if I had done the right thing. I'm sure we have all had those days!

I found that it was so important to set goals—goals for my classes, goals for my students and goals for how I was going to keep improving and learning the art of teaching. Writing everything down (or nowadays putting it all into the computer) kept me where I needed to be, and helped measure my progress and success. This is something that I always encourage teachers to do. You must be organized—have lesson plans, plans for choreography, plans on ways to test the students. Also make a plan for yourself personally because that will affect your success in life and as a teacher.

You are a business owner!

As a dance teacher, you are the CEO of your own independent company. As such, you must be able to negotiate with your employers, and show them that you are dependable, eager, and that you have the patience of a saint! Let them see that you have qualifications that will help their students to improve. You are a business person, something very important to understand. It will help put you in a good position with any employer.

Take a good look at where you are as a teacher. Health is extremely important for any instructor, but I would say almost more important for a dance teacher. What we do requires physicality and endurance. Are you happy with where you are currently teaching? Do you have a good and positive relationship with your employers and students? Do you keep up with the latest trends? Are you doing any kind of ongoing education as a dance teacher? All of these questions are important for you to ask yourself. If answered truthfully, they will help determine where you need to be as a teacher.

As dance teachers, we have to be many things. We need to satisfy our employers by being the best that we can be. We need to satisfy our students by helping them to achieve their goals. And we need to satisfy their parents who are paying us to do so. We must be in a very good place mentally to withstand everyone's moods and to remain positive at all times! We want to be creative enough to come up with choreography that everyone thinks is "cool." We also want enough technical knowledge to give students a sufficient vocabulary and the steps they need to achieve their success. Plus we must do it all with a smile! Make no mistake, every class you teach is a performance, and that smile and sense of humor is what makes it all come together. If you have never been a performer, I recommend that you hone in to those performance skills, and if you have performed, you will know exactly what I mean. Whether you have been a professional performer or not, it's safe to say that all dance teachers have performed at one time or another in their lives. Search back to those moments, and remember how it felt and what you did. Bring those skills into the dance studio.

Balance your strengths and weaknesses.

I suggest you sit down and make lists of your strengths and weaknesses. No matter your profession, it is enlightening to do this. You need to know how you can strengthen your strengths and improve your weaknesses. If you feel unhappy where you are teaching, make a list of places where you would like to teach and start sending out your resume. At my studio, I constantly look at new teachers because although I have a wonderful faculty, life sometimes forces us to make changes. It is always good to be prepared. Research places that offer teacher training near you, and plan to attend in the months when the studios are closed. Make a point of planning personal time, getting-away time, so that you can recharge and stay in a positive frame of mind. Just as we must inspire our students, so we must become newly inspired to give the best possible focus and quality attention that those around us need to receive from us.

In this book, we will help you find ways to become increasingly successful as a teacher and more confident in dealing with the varied people you'll encounter in this field.

Envisioning your life as a dance teacher in the most positive light will help you to find happiness throughout your journey. Sometimes the journey may seem very unrewarding and at other times, quite the opposite. But it will help if you take it one day at a time and look to your eventual destination with anticipation of great things to come.

Bravo! Act Three Curtain Calls

Remember these things:

- You truly do not only teach the art of dance, but also the art of life!
- You are a dance teacher, a member of a very honorable group, and you provide an amazing service to children and their parents every time you teach
- Being adaptable and keeping your mind open to the new and different will go a long way in your continued development as a teacher
- It's immensely satisfying when you see how much you help your students to improve
- You need to be organized and make a plan for yourself, because that will affect your success in life and as a teacher
- As a dance teacher, you are the CEO of your own independent company
- Health is extremely important for a dance teacher
- Every class you teach is a performance, and your smile and sense of humor make it all come together
- You need to know how you can strengthen your strengths and improve your weaknesses
- Involve yourself in some kind of teacher training in the months when the studios are closed
- Envisioning your life as a dance teacher in the most positive light will help you to find happiness throughout your journey

NOTES

Chapter Two

Your Feet on the Path

Your Feet On The Path—Act One: **Steve Sirico**

> "Treat people as if they were what they ought to be and you help them become what they are capable of becoming."
>
> —*Johann Wolfgang von Goethe*

Think about it—teachers play many roles to students. To students, you are coach, mentor, surrogate parent, counselor, motivational speaker, life coach and confidante. They rely on your words of encouragement and are hopefully motivated by your critiques. You hold the keys to helping each student you touch. You can help students grow, and you can also inhibit their growth if you are not careful. Your effect on your students is infinite and currently unknown. You may shape the way that they advance in their careers, the way they will behave as partners and spouses, and the way they will raise their kids. As I am writing this, I realize you may be feeling a bit like Atlas right now, bearing the weight of the world on your shoulders. Wow—this just in: Teaching is a lot of work and involves a lot of responsibility.

With that in mind, you may have times when you question yourself and the validity of what you are teaching. You may wonder how you can get to the next level as a teacher. Questions of doubt may pop up in your mind. You may feel that you are stuck in the spot you are in, year after year, and you don't see any way to progress. I recommend that you think again. The great news is that you do not ever have to be in neutral, and you do not need to be stuck in one place or at one level. When you question your progress, or lack thereof, it is only normal—part of the process that can get you moving forward.

See if you have asked yourself any of these questions:
Am I a good teacher?
Am I giving my students all they need?
How can I get more out of them?
Why am I not reaching that student?
Do my students like and respect me?
What can I do to give my students more?
How can I do a better job?

If you have asked yourself these questions or other similar questions from time to time, the great news is that you most definitely are a good teacher!

Why? Because you care! If you didn't care you would never question what you are doing. Great teachers are made because they work at it. They understand that what you know today will be only better once you learn how to impart that knowledge with tomorrow's new advances. It is one of the things I enjoy most about teaching. I have never stopped learning! How boring would it be to learn something once and do that for the rest of your life. Don't forget that you need to constantly refresh yourself with new ideas and techniques. It is a BIG key to helping you stay fresh mentally.

But knowledge only takes you so far. The key is that students don't care about how much you know until they know about how much you care. Read that line over and over again. Remember, it is not what you know—it's what you can get your students to know that counts. That is why I chose the quote to start this chapter. It is about mindset. Once you get your students in the right mindset, they will respond accordingly. As teachers, we also must have the right mindset. It is contagious, and your actions will dictate how your students receive your instruction.

A teacher who loves learning earns the right and the ability to help others learn

Here is the reality: To be a great teacher, you must continue to be a great student. I can honestly say that through the years, my students have taught me a lot. The key to being a great teacher is to help your students exceed their expectations. Seeing the potential in each and every student is pivotal to helping him or her achieve outstanding results. Isn't that what teaching really is all about? A great teacher will inspire and entertain, and recipients won't even realize that they have learned a ton! Oh, yes, there will be times we need to be a bit tough, but not because we want to intimidate, only because we want to give a push to help someone move upward. If your push knocks the student down, then you are not helping that person move in the right direction. Finding the right way to correct students and get them to listen is one of the most challenging parts of teaching. It will be individualized for each student.

> "Tell me and I forget. Teach me and I remember. Involve me and I learn."
>
> —*Benjamin Franklin*

This is another quote that I just love. It is so easy for students to fall through the cracks. You know who they are. The shy ones with little or no self-esteem; the ones who hide from your sight for fear you may notice them. Those are the ones we must reach, as well. Those are the ones who will test your metal as a teacher. Those are the ones who will teach you valuable lessons on teaching! Involving all of your students in your classes will always be a challenge. But you will stand apart from the rest once you master this piece of teaching. Let's face it—teaching the good students is easy for the most part. But teaching the ones who struggle is your real test. Keeping students motivated, involved and engaged will be the most important part of teaching. The trick will be to keep yourself motivated, involved and engaged in teaching. Your students will follow your lead!

Check list for being a great teacher:

- **Always be on time and prepared for class**. If you don't check this one off all the time the other points on this list won't matter!
- **Maintain a professional relationship with your students, their parents and your employer**. This is such a big part of how to receive proper treatment as a professional. You wouldn't want to see your doctor behaving unprofessionally. Make sure to maintain your status at all times.
- **Give your students material that makes them look good**. When it comes to choreography and class work, the most important

part is not necessarily giving your students what you as a teacher would like to do but giving them material that makes them shine. Remember, if they don't look good, you don't look good!

- **Have goals for yourself and your students.** Years pass quickly and if you aren't careful, in five years, you'll still be where you are today. Write down the goals you set for yourself as a teacher. Go ahead and be bold! Sit down and think about all of your dreams and aspirations. Make a goal chart for each class you teach. You can share that goal chart with your class as the year progresses.
- **Push, but never demoralize or deflate.** I believe that, as a teacher, there will be times when you must be tough, demanding and hard on your students. However, you must build trust and understanding with them before you can do so. Never intimidate or put down your pupils. That will only backfire.
- **Dress for success**. It is important to look the part. Always have the clothes you teach in look good, and always look well-groomed. If you look good, your students will want to look good.
- **Keep yourself updated on what is new and what is happening in your industry**. Stay fresh in your field. Be sure to attend industry events such as: conferences, seminars and teacher-training schools. There are also great online resources like Dance Teacher Web.com, Dance Informa.com and Dance Teacher's Online.com
- **Communicate with your employer.** If you want to do something new or are not happy about something at the studio, it only makes sense to communicate with the person who can make a change. Refrain from airing your thoughts to fellow employees, parents or students. They can't help resolve issues or help you achieve your desired outcome.
- **Be ready for change.** Most people do not like change. Change can be uncomfortable, but it is inevitable. Adaptability will be one of your biggest assets.
- **Have fun, be easy to work with and passionate.** Let's face it, divas don't last. Who wants to deal with all the drama? If you are

easy to work with, have fun no matter what you teach, and love what you do, you will be successful!

So there you have it! If you have check marks next to each of these points, keep up the great work. If not, don't stress! Life is a journey and so is teaching. The teacher I am today is vastly changed from the one I was twenty-five years ago. I pass these tips on to you from what I have learned along the way. Remember the only person who can really effect change in you is YOU!

Check out this quote by Robert Maxwell (taken from a Chinese proverb) about teaching:

If You Want Happiness: *"If you want happiness for an hour, take a nap. If you want happiness for a day, go fishing. If you want happiness for a month, get married. If you want happiness for a year, inherit a fortune. If you want happiness for a lifetime, help others, be a teacher!"*

Keep in mind that teaching is all about the student. You can't ever go wrong if you put the students first.

> Plan Purposefully, Prepare Plentifully, Proceed Positively, Pursue Persistently!
>
> —*William Arthur Ward*

The teacher's mantra!

Bravo! Act One Curtain Calls

Remember these things:

- Teachers are everything to their students
- You have the keys in your hands to help each student you touch
- To question your progress is only normal and part of the process that can get you moving forward
- As a teacher you never stop learning
- You need to constantly refresh yourself with new ideas and techniques
- Students don't care about how much you know until they know about how much you care
- It's not what you know but what you get your students to know
- Get your students in the right mindset and they will respond accordingly
- To be a great teacher you must continue to be a great student
- Seeing the potential in each and every student is the key to helping them achieve outstanding results
- Keeping students motivated, involved and engaged is the most important part of teaching
- Give your students material that makes them look good
- Push but never demoralize or deflate
- Be ready for change
- Have fun, be easy to work with
- Be passionate about who you are and what you do
- Plan Purposefully, Prepare Plentifully, Proceed Positively, Pursue Persistently!

Your Feet On The Path—Act Two: **Angela D'Valda Sirico**

> "A hundred years from now it will not matter what kind of car I drove, what kind of house I lived in, how much money I had in the bank . . . but the world may be a better place because I made a difference in the life of a child."
>
> —*Forest Witcraft*

You are now on your chosen path of being a dance teacher. Did you really choose to be a teacher or did it, in a way, choose you? People arrive at the teaching profession for different reasons and from different paths. When you were a child did you dream of being a teacher or did it just sort of come upon you that this might be something that you could do? Did you go to college to become a teacher or did you become one because you happened to be in the right place at the right time? Why you are a teacher is important because, by understanding the reason or reasons behind your decision, you can keep progressing. You can become a great teacher, someone who inspires and can engage students in such a way that they will always remember your lessons and how you delivered them.

So what is the secret to "greatness"?

There are many answers to this question, but I think probably the most important factors are having a passion for what you do and communicating that passion to others effectively. Most of us have had teachers at school or in dance to whom we just could not relate. We hopefully also have had teachers who inspired us and made us feel special. I remember as a very young child I had a dance teacher whose name was Miss Dorothy Watkins. I absolutely loved her classes and remember being fascinated with the skirts she wore to teach in. They always moved beautifully when she demonstrated. Miss Watkins would always make the classes so much fun and was tremendously encouraging to me as a young girl.

I have had other dance teachers who made an impact on my life. Ivor Meggido taught me jazz for the first time when I was attending Arts Educational School in England. He encouraged me to study in New York with Matt Mattox, who had a huge influence on my dancing. Fred Favorite and Bob Devoye were instrumental in helping us put our adagio act together, and then gave us our first job as an act in the show that they were producing.

We owe them a lot. There were others who affected my life and direction in a very positive way, and I am eternally grateful to them for helping me realize my passion as a dancer and giving me insight into what makes a great teacher. I really don't believe that you start out as a great teacher. You become one if you are willing to work at it and understand that it is a journey that teaches you something new at every turn.

Teaching can be such a rewarding job, but it can also be extremely daunting and draining if either you or your students do not have the right mindset. Perhaps the most important point to keep in mind is that the role you play in the students' lives should be an enjoyable one. How much more fun is it to teach with humor and a smile than with a harsh attitude? Of course, there needs to be discipline, and children need and want boundaries, but they will want to respond in a positive way when they feel encouraged and challenged. If you set high expectations, your students will generally do their best to live up to them. As dance teachers, we often spend more time with our students than their parents do. This gives us an opportunity to help them become good dancers and happy, well-adjusted people. Students want to know that you care about them, not only as a dancer but as a person.

I love this quote by Carl Jung:

> "One looks back with appreciation to the brilliant teachers but with gratitude to those who touched our human feelings. The curriculum is so much necessary material, but warmth is the vital element for the growing plant and for the soul of the child."

The truth is that each class is full of students who are all individuals, both in character and in the way they learn. So you must develop individual ways to help them to learn and to bring out their characters. Sometimes, there are so many complex individuals that you can get overwhelmed. You may question whether you are getting through to a few, thinking perhaps that they need more of one thing and less of the other. Or maybe their mindsets are just not where they need to be. Finding ways for students to think positively and creatively is, in my opinion, the most valuable part of my job. Once students have the right mindset, the sky is the limit. So often, students feel that despite their efforts they are incapable of executing steps correctly. In my class, when a student is having difficulty with a particular step, I like to ask that person to try the step alone. I say to him or her, "Why am I asking you to do this step? Simply, because you can!" Ninety-nine times out of 100, the student manages to execute the step well—maybe for the first time ever. I like to show students that they truly can do it. When they do, and see that the method works, it is as if the sun has come out. Realizing that the mind is stronger than the body is a wonderful lesson to be learned.

> "Once children learn how to learn, nothing is going to narrow their minds. The essence of teaching is to make learning contagious, to have one idea spark another."
> ***A great quote by Marva Collins***

In my experience, once students see that I care about them as dancers and as people, I always get better results. When children feel unnoticed or unappreciated, they tend to withdraw into themselves more. It is very difficult to get them to open up their minds and be willing to learn. Even the most untalented student has something to offer. By focusing on that, rather than what they don't have, a much better and more productive teacher-student relationship will blossom.

Teaching is a fascinating profession, and what I love most is the constant learning for myself. I enjoy the fact that I need to stay interested in the material and in my students. In a way, I view it as a jigsaw puzzle. I know what the picture is, but it is how I put it all together that counts! By having a good plan for my classes, whether on paper on in my head, I know that I am giving the students the best of my knowledge and encouraging them to venture and discover beyond that.

Sometimes, I walk into class and the entire plan goes out the window. In the very first exercise, I see something that needs addressing—and so I do via the content of the class. Could I have done that when I first started teaching? Probably not, and I would not have had the confidence then that I have now. It didn't make me a bad teacher, but simply one who was not as experienced. I love to pass on my love of movement to my students. I like to help them understand that people have danced from the beginning of time as an expression of their joy or sadness, and that the technique we give them in every class can be used to show, through their movement, their own love of dance. I enjoy giving my students the chance to work at the highest level possible for them and to understand that life is too short for hard work not to also be fun.

A dancer's career is short, but a teacher's can literally last a lifetime.

We do, I believe, have a code of ethics as does any professional. For me they are as follows:

1. Always maintain professionalism, from student to parent to employer
2. Be consistent, in classes and in the way you present yourself
3. Always be reliable
4. Commit to ongoing dance teacher education
5. Develop a love of movement for all your students
6. Show your students that you care about them and how they learn
7. Stay positive and inspiring
8. Keep laughter and fun in all classes from beginner to the most advanced
9. Stay in good communication with your employer
10. Remember you are the CEO of your teaching business

Above all, remember that you have the ability to help many children become good dancers and lead valuable lives. What a terrific privilege and honor it is to know that so many children will pass through our lives—even the ones who seem to have no direction. In fact, when you show a child how to think for him- or herself, to move in a new direction, to see that light go on when he or she "gets it"—what a wonderful feeling! We belong to a community that gives children skills and tools for life and dance, and for that we should be celebrated.

Bravo! Act Two Curtain Calls

Remember these things:

- Have a passion for what you do and communicate that passion to others.
- You don't start out as a great teacher. You become one—if you are willing to work at it and understand that it is a journey that teaches you something new at every turn.
- The role you play in the students' lives should be an enjoyable one.
- Develop discipline. Children need and want boundaries.
- If you set high expectations, students will generally do their best to live up to them.
- Every student wants to know that you care about him or her, not only as a dancer, but as a person.
- We must constantly find ways to teach our students to think positively and creatively.
- The realization that the mind is stronger than the body is a wonderful lesson to be learned.
- Once students feel you care about them as dancers and as people, you always get better results.
- Help students to understand that life is too short for hard work not to also be fun.
- A dancer's career is short, but a teacher's can last a lifetime.
- Keep laughter and fun in all classes, from beginner to the most advanced.
- You can show children how to think for themselves and have a direction to go toward.
- You belong to a community that gives children skills and tools for life.

Your Feet On The Path—Act Three: **Robert Landau**

> "The mediocre teacher tells, the good teacher explains, the superior teacher demonstrates, the great teacher inspires."
>
> —*William Arthur Ward*

What makes a great teacher? They are definitely few and far between. But without them, teaching wouldn't be the fine art that it is and students wouldn't be motivated to achieve greatness. A great teacher makes a difference to the student and to the class as a whole. Great teachers make a difference to the school, which then makes a difference to the surrounding community, which makes a difference to its resident state, which then in turn makes a difference to the country, which makes a difference to the world at large. And it all starts with you!

The One and Only, Mr. Uyeda!

There was excitement in the air. Everyone could feel it. Mr. Uyeda's fourth-grade class was buzzing about the assignment he had given the day before. It was time for students to make brief presentations about how they would run the country if they were President of the United States. Looking around, you wouldn't think anyone was nervous about making a presentation in front of the class, but one little boy was. He was VERY nervous. So nervous in fact that he started to sweat, which lead to continuous shaking and then to extreme dryness of the mouth. He didn't know how he was going to make it through. He made sure to position himself at the end of the presentation line so he could delay the inevitable as much as possible. This wasn't fun. He just wished he could go home and forget about the whole thing. Escapism? Oh yes, to the nth degree! No one told him fourth grade was going to be like this. This truly was the worst ever. If he just could have sneaked into class that day, totally unseen, things might have been better. But for now, there wasn't a worse day in school that he could remember.

"I would bring total peace to the world," one student proudly said. Another confidently marched to the front of the room, positioned herself front and center, smiled, and said, "As President, I would make sure there was food for everyone. No one would ever be hungry, ever!" This caused the entire class to erupt in wild supportive applause. "Free video games for everyone," another student said to rousing cheers from the rest of the class.

Mr. Uyeda smiled broadly because the desired result of his assignment was now being realized by his class. Fun was being had by all in the name of creativity and imagination. But not all students had their time in front of the class. Guess who was left? When the rest of the class realized that only one person now remained, it suddenly got so quiet, you could hear a pin drop. All eyes now focused on the one remaining student, who was just sitting there, totally terrified.

"There's only one student left. So let's hear from him now, shall we?" Mr. Uyeda said, hoping to provide a little motivation for the boy to rise, come forward and deliver. No go! The boy just sat there, miserably wishing he could be somewhere else, anywhere else, at this moment in time. "If I only had a magic wand, this is the time I'd use it. I'd wave it, and all of this would go away and I'd be in my room at home," the boy thought. Mr. Uyeda then said to the class, "Everyone, let's give him a big round of applause so he can share his ideas and views with the rest of us." At first, not one student would clap for the boy, which of course, made him feel even worse —if that was at all possible! A few minutes later, the class applauded as the boy rose to his feet and slowly made his way to the front of the room. Once in position he looked out and saw a sea of eyes looking back at him with what seemed to be hatred and judgment. "OK, I'll just say what I have to say in the best way I can, and you know what? They'll love it!" the boy thought to himself. He looked out at everyone again, took a deep breath and prepared to share his first words. A few seconds seemed like two months to the boy. He decided to just "go for it," and said, "Umm . . . if I were President, I'd send love to everyone and, and make them smile!" Another few seconds passed—it seemed like two months—before the class reacted. Then, as if someone had flipped some switch somewhere, the entire class burst into loud, jeering laughter. The boy was taken by surprise and felt as if he were two inches tall. To make matters worse, now various members of the class started teasing him. The negative energy grew to a fevered pitch. The boy wanted to run as far from this horrific real-life nightmare as possible, but was paralyzed with hurt, fear and utter despair. The bullying energy had never been this bad and this pervasive.

All at once, Mr. Uyeda, from where he was standing at the side of the classroom spoke up. "Everyone, be quiet, and be quiet now. I don't want to hear anything from anyone. I'm extremely disappointed that you all took it upon yourselves to react that way to what was just shared with you. Can I ask you what he did to deserve your negative and hateful reaction? Nothing, I suspect! All of you shared your wish today, he just shared his. Did he react that way to what each of you had to say when you were up there? Listen everyone and listen well—the boy you see standing before you may be very hurt by your unwarranted reactions, but one day I guarantee you, he'll be doing things that you can only dream of. Being special and wonderfully unique is something to be proud of. Even if this isn't totally realized yet in all of us, it's something to respect and learn from. Shame on all of you! That wasn't the point of this assignment. One day, what this beautiful boy said moments ago will make sense to you. It's meaningful, deep and profound. How come any of YOU didn't come up with it?"

The class was silent. Once again, you could have heard a pin drop. The boy was so full of emotion that he wanted to burst into a million pieces. But instead, he quietly left the front of the class and sat back in his seat, way in the back of the class. He knew deep within that something changed that afternoon. Something had shifted, but what it was, he hadn't the slightest idea.

In case you haven't figured it out, that little boy was me. I will never forget that day. As horrible as it was, the sun did eventually come out because for the very first time, who I was—my energy, my essence, my being as an individual, was finally acknowledged and understood. Even if I didn't understand it fully at the time, someone else did. In all of five minutes, I went from being completely torn down to being lifted up as a positive example for all to see and learn from. There was something different about me, this I always knew. But it took Mr. Uyeda to bring it out of me. I will never forget him. Mr. Uyeda understood me in ways that few others ever did. It was as if he got into my being and knew exactly who I was. Not only that, who he knew I was seemed to be totally OK with him; he stood behind me when no one else would. He was the teacher that meant the most to me in my life and believe me, I've had a lot of amazing teachers in my time. Mr. Uyeda is why I'm able to appreciate who I am today. Because of him, I'm never afraid to stand before a group of people and say what I feel moved to say. He helped me realize that I have an important message to share, and it's something I should never be afraid or ashamed of. My message is me, and for this I will always be indebted to Mr. Uyeda. All of this from a fourth-grade teacher!

Do you have a similar story concerning a teacher you'll never forget? So many of us do. Think of how much time you and I spent in classrooms growing up. We think we lived at home, but in reality, our homes were in the schools we attended for so many years. Our teachers became our makeshift parents. They were our mothers and fathers during the day, and our true parents took over the job in the evenings and on weekends. Just as you might have a parent or family member you'll never forget, you probably have a teacher who has meant just as much or more.

Why share this story with you? Because anytime you doubt that you have an effect on students' lives, think again. Mr. Uyeda was a great teacher, and you know what? So are you! Don't believe me? Think over your time as a teacher. Can you think of any students whose lives you've changed for the better? It's that moment of change that I want you to think about. Just as Mr. Uyeda did in that moment when he said what he did to his class of doubters, it may have taken one fleeting moment for you to change a student's life forever.

So what is it about a teacher that can make such a profound difference in the life of a student? There are multiple answers to this question, but first and foremost is this: It is teaching that moves students, comes from one place and one place only—your heart! If your heart isn't in it, it ain't gonna happen! If your heart isn't in it, your students will somehow sense this and you'll instantly feel them disengage. Do your students sometimes seem disinterested in what you have to say? Consider the possibility that it might what you are sending out rather than something they might be going through.

If you think teaching from the heart is difficult and requires years of study, think again. As a lover of dance, your passion and creativity should always be at the forefront of any dance-related effort. As a teacher, your passion, creativity and sheer love of the art form, if it's genuine, is a prime motivator to the students you teach. As you lead your classes day after day, you intuitively know when an important moment comes along, one offering a chance to make a difference in a student's life. If you feel the opening is there, go for it! Don't hold back. As long as what you impart is in keeping with the true reason you are there, you, too, can save the day for a student in need. Saving the day might in turn mean saving a life.

The event I shared with you from the fourth grade was a true "ah-ha moment" for me, one of my first. But it's the one I'll never forget. Never shy away from giving a student of yours an ah-ha moment. It could just be the moment of profound change. It doesn't only make you a great teacher, it makes you unforgettable. Just ask Mr. Uyeda.

Bravo! Act Three Curtain Calls

Remember these things:

- Making a difference in a student's life starts with you.
- Being special and wonderfully unique is something to be proud of.
- You have the ability to learn the very essence of students' beings and to truly know who they are—even if they don't.
- We think we live at home but in reality, our homes are in the studios or schools where we teach.
- Teaching that moves students comes from your heart.
- Your passion and creativity should always be at the forefront of any dance-related effort.
- You can save the day for a student in need. Saving the day might in turn save a life.

NOTES

Chapter 3

On the Way to Work

On the Way to Work—Act One: **Angela D'Valda Sirico**

> "Don't aim for success if you want it; just do what you love and believe in, and it will come naturally."
>
> —*David Frost*

Most of us become teachers because we desire to pass on our accumulated knowledge and offer our students the inspiration and tools needed to succeed in both their lives and in dance. Sometimes, it is easy to forget that we love to teach because so many roadblocks can strip us of our passion—if we permit them to do so. We must constantly remind ourselves of why we chose teaching. Each day, we reignite the passion that set the whole thing in motion in the first place. Passion truly is a gift, and I for one, feel so grateful for a burning desire to succeed and to follow on the path that dance has led me since early childhood. I know that my success depends upon my interactions, both personally and professionally, at each stage of my life. It is sustained by my belief in myself and the belief others had in me.

Success as a person and a teacher starts from the moment you wake up in the morning and continues in the choices you make throughout the day. The first thing I do when I wake up is to say, "Thank You!" Thank you for being healthy, thank you for working in a profession I love, and thank you for my family and friends who give me daily support. Oh, and I do also say thank you for my two amazing pups, Bert and Frasier! Even if I wake up feeling tired or sore or just plain miserable, I have learned that I have the power to not permit myself to wallow in negativity. I can lift my spirits so that I feel ready to face whatever the day may bring. Trust me, this knowledge did not happen overnight and there are still days when I have to make a greater effort to push myself up, but being grateful for what I have and knowing that I can have a great day if I so choose, has helped me on many occasions.

On the way to work

No matter what mode of transportation you use to get to work—by car, train, bus or simply walking—it is a moment to have time to yourself. I often use my commute to organize my brain into the right frame of mind by the time I arrive at the studio to teach my classes. I have learned during my adult life that the mind is definitely stronger than the body and that I can control my mind to either think positively or negatively. We all have days when we are feeling tired or out of sorts or just plain unmotivated. We wouldn't be human if we didn't. On days when I am not really feeling that great or not in the mood to teach, I try to give myself a task to accomplish. Perhaps I need to sit down and listen to music so that I have the right material for choreographing. Or maybe I look at my class plans and decide what my students most need to work on. Just the act of sitting down and making a plan for the day seems to get me going. Music will always motivate me because I love it, and like all dance teachers, I want to make movement to it. If I don't have the extra time in my day, I know that I can use my travel time to create in my thoughts, on paper or on my computer the content for my students. Some people view travel time as a waste. I view it as undisturbed time to think!

As dance teachers, we must continually inspire and positively reinforce our students. We want and need them to be in the right mindset, and quite often they are not getting that help from their parents. So it is up to us to show them the way. As with anything, you lead by example, and so it is vitally important for you to find balance and harmony for yourself and ensure you have the strength to lead in a positive way. Everyone has his own, individual way of staying positive. Personally, I start by not keeping constantly negative people around me. People who always look at the negative side of things are generally not very happy. Consequently, they love to have as many like-minded people around them as possible. Negativity breeds more negativity, and we have enough of a job keeping ourselves and our students' positive without being bogged down by a bunch of negative thoughts! It is also important that we present ourselves in a positive light to our employers and our student's parents.

Dance gives us numerous ways to develop our self-discipline—for example, the repetition of exercises, the drive and determination to succeed, and the willingness to take chances and go out on a limb if necessary. These practices develop good habits that are useful to us as teachers and adults. When we live them, we can pass our experiences on to our dance students.

So many people fear failure or making a necessary move. Fear paralyzes them and prevents them from moving forward. Again, dance really does teach us about failure, simply because you probably will fail over and over as a dancer before you master the best ways to perform.

Teaching can be intimidating if you do not feel confident about yourself. How many times have you stepped into your classroom and felt critical or negative waves circulating around the room?

The question is what do you do to combat that kind of reaction?

Do you have a plan that you can put into place?

Or do you take command and turn it all around to a positive energy?

For some people this is instinctive, but for others it is difficult. The good news is it can be done. The real solution to any attitude problem is YOU. You are like the conductor of a symphony orchestra. You can make all the different personality groups come together in harmony, as you would with all the different musical instruments—as long as you are in harmony with yourself.

Do you enjoy your classes?

Do you have fun with your students?

If you do, they will enjoy what you teach them and will look forward to studying with you regularly. If things are not running as smoothly as you prefer, remember that you have the power to change things until you find a way that works best. Good preparation will always help build self-confidence in whatever you do.

> "The task of the excellent teacher is to stimulate 'apparently ordinary' people to unusual effort. The tough problem is not in identifying winners; it is in making winners out of ordinary people."
>
> —*K. Patricia Cross*

As I prepare myself for the day, I hope that by following a certain code of ethics I can help all of my students achieve greatness in one way or another. It is easy to help those tremendously gifted students look good. But finding the gift that lies in each child and helping him or her achieve some level of success—that is the most rewarding. Don't misunderstand me. I love to work with students who pick up the most complicated technique and who make everything I give them look good. But how challenging to see a student who struggles with technique finally grasp and master choreography when he could not possibly have done that a year ago. To see that self-confidence build and the light shine in those eyes is reward enough!

Albert Einstein has a wonderful quote:

"It is the supreme art of the teacher to awaken joy in creative expression and knowledge."

It is this that makes it all worthwhile for me—and why I continue to teach. I have had students from each end of the spectrum, and always will. Each day is a challenge, and tells me how vitally important it is to set my mind in the right direction as I go to teach each day. I do not like mediocrity, and I strive for excellence whenever possible. It's not always easy, and in fact, sometimes it is downright difficult!

Success guidelines for dance teachers

*Be Passionate
*Be Punctual
*Be Prepared
*Be Inspiring
*Be Willing to Learn

If you can follow these guidelines, you will be an excellent teacher and a happy one, too! Your students and their parents will appreciate your efforts, your employers will do what's needed to keep you with them, and I am sure, your personal life will be enriched by the balance and wisdom that you bring to your life and those of others.

Bravo! Act One Curtain Calls

Remember these things:

- Remind yourself why you became a teacher. Ignite the passion that set the whole thing in motion in the first place
- Success as a person and a teacher starts from the moment you wake up each day and continues in the choices you make for yourself each day
- You have the power to reject wallowing in negativity, to lift up your spirits, and to be ready to face whatever the day may bring
- You can control your mind and whether you think positively or negatively
- It is very important for us to find balance and harmony within ourselves in order to have the strength to lead in a positive way
- Negativity only breeds more negativity
- If things are not running as smoothly as you would like, always remember that you have the power to change things around
- Don't settle for mediocrity. Strive for excellence whenever possible

On The Way to Work—Act Two: **Robert Landau**

> "Learn from the past, set vivid, detailed goals for the future, and live in the only moment of time over which you have any control: now!"
>
> —*Denis Waitley*

The alarm sounds. Its annoying and continuous beeping tears through the wonderful sleep state you've managed to achieve all night. You forcefully open one eye and your alarm clock starts to come into focus. It's 6 a.m., and just like every other day, it's time to get up and get ready. "How monotonous!" you think. Something inside you doesn't even want to move an inch. You are snug and comfy under your covers, and you want to stay, luxuriating in that amazing warmth all day. "I'm not going in. They can do it all without me. Somehow it'll just work out. I'm just not in the mood!" you say, hoping that this day, like all others, would just go away. You then decide to muster every last ounce of energy you have and put one foot on your bedroom floor, then the other. Now it's time to lift yourself up and out of bed so you can balance your body on your feet as they, ever so slowly, carry you to the bathroom. You do your best to get ready for the upcoming day. "If I could only just back track a number of steps and get back into that warm and inviting bed, no one would even miss me!" you think. You decide that, as tempting as that might sound, you've got a whole string of classes you have to teach today, and students, like it or not, are depending on you.

After making the worst breakfast ever known to man, you get dressed, get into your car and drive off to work. "Why do I even need to keep my eyes open? I've driven this darn route for so long now the car probably knows how to get there even better than I do!" And that's just where your thoughts start! If anyone happened to have been serving up a lethal dose of negativity this morning, it seems to be coming from you at this particular moment.

All at once your thoughts shift to focusing on even more negativity. This time it's in the form of what might happen once you walk into the dance studio. "Christine at the desk won't even look up to greet me because she's mindlessly gossiping to some of the other staff about what went down yesterday or the day before. Man, I even hate the smell of that place. Not that there's anything offensive about the smell, it just reminds me of that studio in particular. Then I'll have to say 'Hello' to all the other teachers—Not! I just don't feel like being nicey-nicey, besides, I absolutely detest Sharon. Can't believe she did that to me two weeks ago. I was the one who came up with that great idea for a theme for our next recital, NOT HER! But would anyone even take a second to believe me? Absolutely not! Who the heck does she think she is? To make matters worse, I don't even want to LOOK at Maryann, just hate the way she runs the place. She doesn't have a clue. It's to the point where I don't even say anything at the all too infrequent staff meetings because no one listens anyway. I hate that place, don't even want to be there. Someone, just shoot me please!"

Does any of this sound familiar? If it does, no need to feel ashamed. We're only human, and we're bound to not feel enthralled with what seems to be happening in various facets of our lives. But here's the question: Do you make yourself a victim of circumstance, or do you deal with it and rise above what might appear to be a bunch of negatives? Or even better, how about this—do you often find yourself being dragged out of the present moment, thinking about things that might occur in the future?

I'd like you to meet a very real part of yourself that you might not even realize is always there: mind-chatter! Mind-chatter is that specific small voice within that chatters away, sometimes at a very constant rate, even when you aren't totally conscious of it. It's the part of you that doubts and warns that something tomorrow might not go as well as you're hoping. Everything and anything having to do with fear is mind-chatter's main reason for being. If you've ever wanted to learn how to meditate, mind chatter is what you hear in your mind that keeps you from making progress in the present moment. Standing back and observing the conversation that goes on within you can be quite interesting, to say the least. Here's an important question for you to consider: If you agree that most of your mind-chatter has to do with future events, do those thoughts that you are thinking have anything to do with the real you?

In this little scenario—where you might have been driving to work, convincing yourself of negative situations sure to occur the moment you walk in the door of your studio—are those thoughts really you? I would venture to answer with an unqualified, resounding, "No." Why? Because a you full of fear isn't the you that you were when you came into this world, and it isn't the you that you really are right here and now. Maybe it's the you that you might think you are, but you are so much more than your fears.

So how do you stop the stream of mind-chatter-infected negativity that so often takes you out of the wonder and goodness of the present moment?

One way to not do it is to think you have to eliminate all traces of negative mind-chatter within. This is a part of you, and will always be there. It's part of being human. When it comes up, just acknowledge it and do something to move on from it. Don't let it overtake you or let it define you. A momentary thought of negativity will pass—if you let it. It needn't stay with you for a prolonged period of time. We don't want to believe that we can control negative thoughts that pop up, but in reality, we are. You have the power to move on from thought patterns that don't serve you. But it's a choice—your choice. No one can get into your mind and make you think any differently than you do right now, except you.

When you have a negative thought come up, acknowledge it, return to your breathing and move on. Think of something else that will get you out of the negative place you just were. Most mind-chatter-type thoughts have to do with an imagined future event. Ask yourself why you'd want to spend so much time thinking about things that haven't even happened yet. Among other things, this takes you out of the present moment. The present moment just 'is.' There's no good or bad in it, it just is. It's like your breath. Your breathing process is neither good nor bad, it just 'is.' Your breathing process has nothing to do with the past or the future, it is always here and now. Anytime you find yourself doing a disservice to yourself and want to move on from dwelling too much on the past or the probable future, focus on your breathing process. It's always in the present. It will take you out of where you were and bring you back to where you should always be. We are always naturally in the present, we are the ones that take ourselves out of that joy and focus on what has or hasn't happened yet.

Another way to look at this is how you'd work with a student who can't seem to catch on to a particular combination that you might be teaching. The rest of the class caught on a long time ago, but every time you want to do the entire routine, that one student can't seem to get past that one rather tricky combination. Think about what you would do to make this situation right. You'd most likely focus on that one student, and lovingly take him or her through the combination, have that person repeat what you are demonstrating and move on to more present matters once he or she has it right. Once the student is confident that he has it down, whenever it gets to that particular part of the routine, he moves through it with ease because you took the time to correct the issue.

So it is with negative mind-chatter. Take the time to acknowledge that you are experiencing a negative thought. Work with it to get it right. Ask yourself how real that negative thought might be, and then move onward. Don't say you'll do it, just do it! There's nothing wrong with having negative thoughts. But thoughts come and go. It's when you invite them to stay that you begin to believe you are the very thoughts that don't serve you.

Think of the sea shore. The tide rushes in and then nature makes sure that it rushes out. It's unnatural to have the tide stay in without an adverse reaction. That would be against every rule of nature, and just it's not how the universe works. So it is with mind-chatter, negativity or fear-based thoughts. The thought comes up, but it also needs to leave just as fast as it came. You can control that. You are the master of your universe. Just make sure the negative thought rolls back out after it has come in.

So what do you do about the studio owner and how he or she runs the place? The only thing you can do is work with your reaction to what you perceive to be the truth. In other words, you have to decide if things are OK enough for you to not let them get to you. If you don't think you can handle what goes on at work, then make a change. Always remember that you can't change other people into to what you want them to be. People are what they think they are. It's how you deal with it that makes the difference.

So the next time you find yourself imagining the future as you're driving to work or laying in bed, not wanting to start your day, smile and know that the thought you just had is fine. But it's not going to overtake you and turn your day sour. You are so much more powerful than that. Acknowledge it and move back to the present moment. You deserve all the good that is destined to come to you. It's like a tide that is rushing in to serve you. Let it in, and don't stand in its way. It's always there to give you exactly what you need. Would you deny what nature has intended for you? The only way that can happen is if you spend too much time focusing on the past or the "supposed" future. Stay here and now, and realize that everything is fine just the way it is. If it doesn't appear to be, don't fret—just work at making it better.

Want to create a great future? It starts by thinking positively about it and not otherwise. Staying anchored in the present moment and feeling darn good about it automatically sets up a great future for your journey. The present positive paves the way for a future that is positive. Just get out of your way when you feel a certain part of you wants to block the flow. It's nature's way!

Bravo! Act Two Curtain Calls

Remember these things:

- Don't make yourself a victim of circumstance. Deal with it and rise above what might appear to be a bunch of negatives.
- Your mind-chatter is not really who and what you are.
- Mind-chatter has nothing to do with the present. It has everything to do with the past or the future.
- A you full of fear isn't the you that you were when you came into this world, and it isn't the you that you really are.
- When mind-chatter comes up, just acknowledge that it's there and get back to the present moment at hand.
- Mind-chatter is only a distraction if you dwell on it and allow it to be so.
- You have the power to move on from thought patterns that don't serve you. It's a choice.
- We are always naturally in the present, we are the ones who take ourselves out of that joy and focus on what has or hasn't happened yet.
- You have to decide if things are OK enough for you to not let them get to you.
- You are so much more powerful than you think you are.
- To create a great future, start by thinking positively.

On the Way to Work—Act Three: **Steve Sirico**

"Theproblemisnottheproblem. Theproblemisyourattitudeabouttheproblem!"
—Captain Jack Sparrow

Do you remember the first time you taught? Take a moment and think back. It may have been some time ago, but I recommend that you reflect back to that time. Now that you have thought about it, I would like to ask you a few questions:

Were you nervous?
Excited?
Over-prepared or underprepared?
Scared or not feeling very confident?

OK, maybe a little of all of the above. But it was the start of a lifelong commitment to teach something that you have a passion for. Now fast-forward to where you are today and you may be surprised at how you have gone from where you were to where you are now. Things can easily get in the way and sidetrack you from being the best you can be. Life gets in the way. Family and friends can get in the way. Your employer and fellow employees can get in the way. Even your students can get in the way. But I believe the biggest obstacle that gets in your way will be YOU!

Chances are that the first time you were on your way to teach, your mind was in a million places. But it was also focused on how your class would go and how your students would receive that information. Now take a moment to think about where your mind goes on your way to teach today. Is it in a good place or are you thinking in a negative pattern? Do all of life's difficulties get in the way of really enjoying your classes? On your way to your school, do you have a cynical view about an issue at your studio or with your students?

It doesn't have to be that way. Cynical and negative thoughts do not produce positive results! This is tricky nowadays because so many people have a negative outlook on work, life and the overall state of affairs. It's hard not to be cynical or negative about the world we live in and the prospect that we have for advancement.

But your classroom is a sanctuary! It is where all of life's issues need to go away—at least for the couple of hours you are teaching! You must keep yourself in check with a positive outlook, and you need to have positive, thought-provoking messages nearby that you can look at to reinforce your thoughts. I highly recommend that you stay conscious of this, so you can toss out any thoughts that are not serving you well. And it all begins when your day begins. The minute I wake up, I try to start my day off on a good note—even if I have an unpleasant task to do or I am feeling a bit tired.

Keep in mind that if you have a problem with your employer or students and you spend an inordinate amount of time thinking about it on your way to your studio, it will start to affect the way you treat everyone.

The key to being in a good place both mentally and physically is **YOU!**

Here is the message: If you don't like the way your students behave or how your employer treats you, then it is up to you to change the environment. If you just accept it, it will never change. If you just go along with it, then you can't complain about it. Complaining about things is about the most negative thing you can do. It will also make the people you touch and express your complaints to feel that they have to commiserate with you. But it won't fix what is wrong!

Here's how to create a positive environment in your class room and beyond!

It all starts and ends with YOU. Yes, it really is in your hands. If you go into the studio brimming with enthusiasm and energy, guess what will be given back to you? Unfortunately the same holds true when you are negative or a downer. I can't tell you how many times I have seen this lead to the downfall of people I have encountered. Don't believe in positive thinking and find it just a bunch of nonsense? Well I recommend that you think again!

Try This!

Try, over the next thirty days, to think in a positive way every time you enter your car to go and teach. Put on some great music or a motivational CD, something that will get you into a good place. Think about what a great profession you practice and what a wonderful job you are doing. Think about the positive impact you have on your students—not just in dance, but in life. When you enter the studio make a point to say hi to everyone and to smile—not a fake one, but one you really feel. Remember: You have just spent time in your car, bus or train ride preparing your mind to feel great about life and your career! When you teach, make sure that you are having a blast. Yes, I said you! Because if you are having a good time, the students will be having one, too! After thirty days, see how the people around you react toward you when they see you. After you see the results, I would bet that you will want to do this for the rest of your life, every single day.

Their perception is their reality!

As teachers, we need to be aware of how our students and employers perceive us. Their perception may not be accurate but it will make a big difference as to how they react to you. It may be that you are sending the wrong messages. It may be that the atmosphere you are creating is not the one you really want to have. Taking a close look at yourself and your teaching style is not always a comfortable thing to do, but I recommend that you do this self-evaluation periodically. Make sure that you are on the right track toward continued development of yourself as the teacher you want to be.

Your classroom environment is created by you.

Read that a few times, and really let it sink in. If you are having a hard time motivating your students, it may be that you don't feel motivated to teach them. If your class is out of control, you are probably facilitating it. If you and your boss are not getting along, it may be that you are carrying baggage into the studio. I have seen many teachers come in at the beginning of the semester with a new attitude, outlook and demeanor—all of a sudden, everything they do is improved and they feel so much better about themselves. It was as simple as changing their thought process. It really does make a BIG difference!

> "It's not your aptitude that determines your altitude, it's your attitude!"
>
> —*Zig Ziglar*

Now let that sink into your head for awhile. The question is how is your attitude? Do you need an attitude adjustment? The good news is that you are in control of your thoughts, acts and deeds!

Look, the reality is that if you are not happy where you are working, you need to get together with your employer and see if you can work it out. If not, it is probably best for all parties that you move on. No one is forcing you to work for that employer. If you are bitter, unhappy and unproductive, who is that really hurting? Mostly your reputation!

There is an old saying that your reputation will precede you.

This is a BIG key for you getting ahead as a teacher and professional. No matter what happens, you must always act and respond as the professional you are. Building a good reputation is something that you create, nurture and build!

Since it gets there first, let the news about you be a headline that reads:

You are a wonderful, caring person who is reliable, professional and top-shelf in every way!

Now how does that sound?

Positive thought-provoking messages!

Hey look, we are all human and sometimes things just push us down, get us down or make us miserable. The key is to have some message that you can look at that will snap you out of it. I love the story of a speaker named Len Brown who has created 360 cards with a motivational quote on each of them. Some he has created and some he has found that really speak to him. He reads the card the minute he wakes up and sticks it in his pocket to review throughout the day. I recommend that you take it another step further and give yourself a positive statement. Try it out, because it works and will help set you on the right track. You may not need a different one for each day, so try out one quote or statement for a week. And see if it helps you when you are having one of those days!

- I am a master teacher and I give my best to each class I teach!
- I believe success occurs when preparation meets opportunity!
- I am a people person. My students and their parents think the world of me. I make a BIG difference in people's lives!
- I expect the best from people and will always give my best!
- Today is the day something great will happen!

- I always meet the right people who can help me reach all of my goals!
- I create great choreography and my students will love my work!

These statements have one mission—to get you into the right frame of mind. Throughout this book, you will see inspiring quotes that also help you get into the right frame of mind. I encourage you to create your own, as well, to get you on the right track and to keep you there. Remember the quote, often attributed to Abraham Lincoln, *"Most people are about as happy as they make up their minds that they want to be."* In other words, don't let outside influences dictate how you will think or feel. Yes, this will be challenging from time to time, but you are in control and you are the one who will determine your happiness.

The key is to be aware of how you think and what goes into your mind. Be careful of whom you associate with and how their attitudes affect you. In his book, *What to Say When You Talk to Yourself,* author Shad Helmstetter notes a study showing that the average eighteen-year-old has been told "no" or "you can't do that" 148,000 times. Now think about how old you are and how many times more you have been told that! The study also shows that seventy-five percent of self talk is negative. And a separate study shows that more than ninety percent of our daily input into our minds is negative. So you must be proactive regarding how you will stay positive and in the right frame of mind.

The evidence is clear. You will become what you think about most. Your success or failure in anything, large or small, will depend upon your programming—what you accept from others, and what you say when you talk to yourself. So make a point today to start off on the right foot. Make your journey to work the best part of your day!

Bravo! Act Three Curtain Calls

Remember these things:

- Things can easily get in the way and sidetrack you from being the best you can be
- Often, the biggest obstacle in your way is you!
- Cynical and negative thoughts do not produce positive results
- The key to being in a good place both mentally and physically is you!
- If you don't like the way your students behave or your employer treats you, then it is up to you to change the environment
- As teachers we need to be aware of how our students and employer perceive us
- Your classroom environment is created by no one else but you
- You are in control of your thoughts, acts and deeds
- Your reputation always precedes you
- You are a wonderful, caring person who is reliable, professional and top-shelf in every way
- Create your own inspiring quote that you can work with each and every day
- Be aware of how you think and what goes on in your mind
- You will become what you think about the most

NOTES

Chapter 4

Under the Stage Lights

Under the Stage Lights—Act One: **Angela D'Valda Sirico**

"The difference between a successful person and others is not a lack of strength, not a lack of knowledge, but rather a lack of will."
—Vince Lombardi

Dance teachers are faced each day with nurturing their students from a technical aspect and more importantly, from a psychological one. The majority of dance teachers do not hold degrees in psychology, yet we need to help our students, especially the teenage ones, with this incredibly important side of their dance training. Our discussions with dancers promote nutritional health, but very often, the psychological side is omitted. Without adequate nurturing in this area, our young students may never realize their true potential as dancers—or as professionals in whatever field they choose.

Teaching students the art of positive thinking and giving them positive reinforcement are keys to success with them—and as a teacher. Our goal is to give our dancers the motivation to come to class, to work hard to achieve higher levels, and to develop the confidence and self-esteem needed to let their creativity flow freely.

Ways to Keep Your Students Motivated

I like to promote healthy forms of motivation, such as emphasizing collaboration with the group and de-emphasizing rivalry, rewarding effort over talent, and showing dancers that they have control over their improvement and work ethic. They learn they are responsible for their ultimate success.

By giving students these tools, you will help them in the classroom, on stage or in whatever profession they decide to embrace. We focus on the joy of dancing—the real reason why any of us dance—and give our dancers feedback on where and how to improve. We don't list their faults and problems. This promotes a healthy and happy feeling among students and in the long run, will make them stronger dancers and human beings.

At the beginning of the year or semester, I like to sit my students down and ask them to write their short- and long-term goals on a piece of paper. I talk to them about their goals and aspirations, and we reflect on what they accomplished the previous year. By looking back, they can see more clearly how they should move toward their hopes and dreams. It helps to revisit these goals halfway through the year, especially if we feel that they are getting down on themselves, to show what progress has been made. Students so often feel very insecure. It is immensely rewarding to help these young people understand their value and realize their dreams through hard work, perseverance and a desire to not give up. I am certain that the majority of dance teachers have reached out to students and taught them to strive for their potential, not just as dancers but as decent human beings.

Probably one of the most important things for students to realize is that by pushing themselves beyond their comfort zone, they will discover that they can achieve things they never believed possible. The path to success is governed by self-discipline, and those individuals willing to do what's needed, even if they don't feel like it at times, will progress and realize their full potential. It is not easy, but the rewards can be great. Only by having that self-discipline and perseverance will they make their dreams come true. Of course, this applies in dance and as a life lesson for whatever path they choose.

The role of a dance teacher is a truly multifaceted one! One minute we are teaching technique; in the next, we are a confidante to a student who needs help with decision-making. We may then find ourselves offering limited medical advice for minor injuries or the flu! The most exciting part of being a teacher of any type, but especially a dance teacher, is that we can help hundreds if not thousands of young people learn to dance and to become confident in their lives. Through dance they learn to work in a team, to think for themselves, to cope in an emergency, to appreciate and understand the results of hard work, and to experience the beauty and joy of an art form that will stay with them for life!

"Optimism is the faith that leads to achievement. Nothing can be done without hope and confidence." —*Helen Keller*

Every student who comes into our classes is looking for the feedback from the teacher that will build hope and confidence. This applies to all of our students—from the least skilled to the most talented. The recreational dancers who come into our classes usually love to dance. Their parents tell stories of how those students put on music and twirl around at home, just savoring the feeling of moving. It is so important to reward or award those students when they make effort or progress. We teach all of our students to receive any correction as they would a gift—with excitement and gratitude! Many students view a correction as a minus, but they learn to see it as something the teacher feels can be corrected, something that will help them achieve a better level. Some students feel "picked on" or embarrassed when corrected. This generally comes from feeling terribly insecure. We can help them understand that our only goal is to help them become stronger in whatever areas need attention. It's just the way you educate them.

Years ago, I really wasn't fond of teaching beginner students, but I taught a weekly beginner ballet class for teens. In the beginning, I would dread this hour, and ask myself, "What on earth can I give them?" They would giggle and talk at a moment's notice. One day, I decided after warming them up that I would have a split contest! Well, of course, most of them could not even come near to a good split. But I showed them the way that I thought was safest and would bring the best results in terms of helping them to stretch out. At first they groaned and moaned because of the pain. I showed them how to take deep breaths and suggested they sing a song while holding the best position they could achieve—anything to get them to stay and not groan! Then I had each student show me a split and I measured how far they were from the floor and wrote it in my book. At the end of class, I commended them on how hard they had worked at their splits. In two months, I told them we would have a true split contest to see who had really been working and improving. That class, simple though it was, became a turning point for me as far as beginner dancers were concerned. We used half the class time, working on this one exercise, but the result was amazing. Instead of walking glumly out of the studio, they all came up to me smiling because now they felt a purpose! Two months later, we held the split contest. It was so gratifying to see how much work they had put into pushing their splits further down. I not only rewarded them with prizes, but I made sure to recognize them individually for their accomplishments. Every bit of this enthusiasm carried over to their work in class, and at the year-end show, they looked really good—with a little help from my choreography!! I managed to win them over and the class just kept on getting bigger. They, of course, grew stronger technically and felt a whole lot more confident. That class taught me a lot about teaching, and since then, I never object to teaching beginners. Even if they don't become great dancers, I know I can help them to be great dance audiences for the future.

Students who are much more advanced can often feel just as insecure, if not more so, than their less-talented peers. They can feel singled out for too many corrections, even though they are corrected for good reasons. They also fear resentment from their fellow students. When you discover an extremely talented student, it is only natural to give them the benefit of all of your knowledge and experience. But it is just as important to recognize the other students with both corrections and some type of acknowledgement, thus keeping a healthy balance.

> "There are no difficult students - just students who don't want to do it your way."
>
> —*Jane Revell and Susan Norman*

The nature of our work means we sometimes deal with difficult students. You know the ones I am talking about—the ones who question your every move, the eye rollers, the talkers, the jealous ones, and the occasional one who just doesn't want to be there! You name it; we have probably all dealt with them from time to time.

In my experience, when children are difficult, they intend to draw attention to themselves and will do whatever they have to do to get it. Sometimes, they just are not relating to the way you are teaching them and need a different approach. That is indeed a challenge for any teacher, especially when you have a good-sized class. But if you do try a different tactic or method, you may find that it stimulates the entire class. Studies have shown the many varieties of ways that children learn. Some need total quiet to absorb the material, while others need some kind of sound to boost their concentration.

Yet another group responds best when doing some kind of movement. The tricky part is determining which group a difficult child belongs in. There really is no right or wrong way to learn, as long as the end result works. But it does help to evaluate the difficult students and see if perhaps they could learn with a different tactic.

> "People's behavior makes sense if you think about it in terms of their goals, needs and motives."
>
> —*Thomas Mann*

Bad behavior is never acceptable, and the students, who show no sense of right or wrong, or exposure to discipline, will need help. Children need to know what your expectations are, because they really do feel much more comfortable when they understand what is acceptable and what is not. Discipline is a part of dance and can transfer over to life very easily. If children are rebellious, rude or disrespectful in class, I let them know that this is not the kind of behavior I expect from them. If the behavior does not change, I sit down with them and their parents to find out what the root of the problem is. If you work in a studio or school, it is wise to let the owner or person in charge know when disruptions occur in your class—policies may differ as to who sits down with the parent. At our studio, if a teacher has problems with a child, we invite the parent in with the child. One of us, the teacher and the family sit down to find a solution. Sometimes, the issue is caused by something or someone in class. But often, it is really all about life at home or school. One of the best ways that I have found to manage an unruly student is to give him or her, a position or task that will put them in the limelight. That generally solves the problem—after all, nine times out of ten, that child is just seeking attention in any way possible.

> "Good teaching is one-fourth preparation and three-fourths theatre."
>
> —*Gail Godwin*

There is no doubt that a good dance teacher needs to be well prepared. Between class plans, continually learning and creating new material for classes and choreography—and being punctual, reliable and looking good—there is also a lot of theatre involved. Each class is a performance, and you are the star. How the performance goes really does depend upon you, and you have the capabilities to make it go whichever way you wish. Just as in a theatre, the show must go on. By teaching our students that very valuable lesson, we are training them to cope and deal with whatever comes along, in dance and in life. What a gift it is to prepare our students with this kind of valuable information. No matter where they go in their lives, they will remember those lessons. They will also remember you for giving them that opportunity to excel.

Bravo! Act One Curtain Calls

Remember these things:

- Teaching students the art of positive thinking and giving them positive reinforcement are the keys to success with them and as a teacher
- Always strive to emphasize collaboration with the group and de-emphasize rivalry
- Keep the focus on the joy of dancing rather than the student's faults and problems
- Ask students to write down their short-term and long-terms goals at the beginning of every semester. Then help them realize their goals
- Keep pushing your students beyond their comfort zones, and they will discover that they are capable of all sorts of things that they never believed they could achieve
- The path to success is governed by self-discipline
- Perseverance and self-discipline help make dreams come true
- Students look for the feedback from the teacher that will give them hope and confidence
- Students who are more advanced can feel just as insecure, if not more so, than their less talented peers
- Since students learn in different ways, look to teach in ways that each student will understand clearly
- Children need to know what your expectations are because they really do feel much more comfortable when they understand what is acceptable and what is not
- Give unruly students a position or task that will put them in the limelight
- Each class you teach is a performance where you are the star
- Teach students that the show must always go on—it is a valuable skill they can use in their lives as they grow

Under the Stage Lights—Act Two: **Steve Sirico**

"A teacher who is attempting to teach without inspiring the pupil with a desire to learn is hammering on cold iron." —Horace Mann

Your success as a dance teacher begins and ends with you! How you get your students involved, and how you keep them engaged, will be a big key to your success. The great news is that you are in control, and you have the power to affect change if you so desire. To get the results you want, you will need a well-thought-out classroom management strategy that includes how to deal with issues, how to give corrections and how to inspire your students when there is a lull.

To inspire your students you must stay inspired!

Teaching over the long haul can be a drain, especially if you are teaching a lot of classes and are pushed to create. One of the toughest things teachers face throughout the season is staying motivated and energized. You are constantly giving, and if you are not careful, you can drain your battery and teaching can become a struggle. One way to keep motivated is to constantly focus on yourself and your needs. This may sound a bit selfish or egotistical, but you are the key to protecting yourself. Don't wait until you get to that tipping point! Know what makes you tick and when you need to relax, what makes you happy outside of dance and when you will make time for you.

That is one of the reasons we created DanceTeacherWeb.com. We have talked to many teachers and they have told us that they feel exhausted and never seem to have any time for themselves. But as we all know, it is more than just ideas and steps. It is about the energy it takes to give and then give some more.

Most dance teachers have to teach many different styles and levels. One minute you are on the floor with preschoolers. Then you are teaching a tap class. Next up is an advanced ballet, jazz or modern class. Sound familiar? The other problem is that dance teachers have a hard time saying no. We do privates, and choreograph for our shows, competition teams or company. So we keep adding more and more to our plate until we feel overwhelmed, exhausted and just slightly resentful. This is something I think we are all familiar with, so the question is what do we do about it?

The first thing I would recommend is to get a daily planner. Write in it everything that you have planned for each day, week and month. Try to build the whole season into the planner.

Next, take a look at where you can and will build in your "down time." Write in your vacations and days off. Then, get a piece of paper and write down at least five things you love to do outside of dance and studio business. It may be a massage, walking your dog, reading a book, taking a swim, playing tennis or golf, getting in the car and going for a day trip. Whatever it is you like to do and find relaxing must go on this list. Now go to your daily planner and see how you can work these things into your schedule. Try to do at least two of these things each month.

Once they are on your schedule, try not to let anything get in the way of this important time. Now when you take a look at you schedule it won't look so bad after all. There is another element that is so important to these "down time" moments. You will find your creativity is enhanced. Some of the best ideas we have come up with have been away from the studio. Your mind is free to think, and sometimes even the smallest or most unexpected idea can ignite your creativity. It really is just giving ourselves that much-needed space that enables us to come up with some great thoughts. It also puts us in the position where we can step back and really look at everything in a better and more positive perspective. We know how hard it is to get away from teaching and not think or talk about everything that is happening at the studio. By giving yourself these times away from your work, it is so much easier to clearly find solutions to any situations.

One very important factor in all of this is to use your "down time" in the most positive way possible. Try not to dwell on any negative things that may be happening. This is not an easy thing to do, but these times away will be of no use to you if that is your focus. When these thoughts come into your mind, you must push them out and refocus on the creative thoughts. If you are having a hard time, then try not to think about dance at all. Get away from it mentally and physically. Have fun trying these methods and see if they make your life a bit easier. The idea is to keep you feeling fresh, motivated and invigorated for the whole season.

Getting the results you want!

I fully believe that your students are a reflection of you. Let that sink in a bit. It may be that you are sending them the wrong message if you are not happy with the results you are getting. It could be as simple as setting certain standards and then helping your students achieve the desired results. If you set the ground rules, and then are willing to enforce them, you will have the kind of students you want. I know this can be a tricky situation if the studio owner who employs you is not on the same wavelength regarding your vision. You may need to sit down to see if you can work this out. It is also challenging if the studio's other faculty let the classroom become a free-for-all. However, I have found that if you expect a certain behavior, even if it is different than what all the other teachers expect, your students will follow your lead.

Classroom management!

The best time to take control of your class is at the start. Set the tone with a list of guidelines, rules, regulations or any other name you want to give it. If presented in a positive way, the class will, for the most part, be happy to follow. Have your students sit down, preferably during their first class, and go over each important item you require. Once you set these guidelines, they will need an occasional review. Once students understand that these exist so to let everyone get the most from the class, they generally get and stay on board.

I also recommend giving them a copy of the rules to take home. This helps their parents understand that your classes are not a free-for-all, and that you are not just a babysitting service. Some of the topics we like to talk about are proper grooming and class attire; no gum chewing in class; no talking (this is a big one to get across); the importance of being on time and paying attention; how to respond to corrections and not to take offense when those are given; and respecting teachers and fellow dancers. I am sure you will come up with your own laundry list of pet peeves when you do this. This is the first step in gaining control of your class and letting its members know that there are boundaries. Students do respect them but will try to push beyond them. You can then revert back to the guidelines and remind them that everyone is expected to follow the rules.

If you don't have the benefit of starting at the beginning of the year, then I would recommend that you teach the first class and make mental notes throughout of things that you don't like or feel that are not conducive to the learning process. Then approach the studio owner and ask if you can set some guidelines to help the students learn faster and have a more pleasurable experience. Next, sit the class down and set the new rules in a fun and upbeat manner. I never like to make it sound like they are going to jail! But I have been to studios where things are so out of control I don't know how the teachers can stand it!

Dealing with the problem child!

Dealing with that one problem child is always a tricky situation and must be dealt with carefully. If a student is reprimanded, I always like to follow it up with a smile shortly afterward so she or he knows it is not personal. Once the child starts to see that you mean business and that the guidelines are to be followed, she or he will start to get with the program! Sometimes parents will come in and say, "You yelled at my child!" You cannot remember doing so and you probably didn't, but the student's perception is that you did. So how you reprimand the student is very important. Try to focus on the behavior not the person. Let the child know before the class is over that you do not hold any grudges! You can achieve this by saying something good about something that the person did well during the class, even if it is a stretch! A smile and reassuring touch on the shoulder can go a long way.

If you are spending too much class time reprimanding, it could be a sign that you are losing the student, and it would be wise to stop the class and calmly go over the guidelines again and again if necessary. Sometimes the only thing left is to dismiss a child from the class. This is always dramatic and will pull the whole class into focus. I would recommend talking to the one that was asked to leave the class before he or she leaves the building. Let the child know that the behavior will not be tolerated and that if it happens again, he or she may not be allowed to take your class anymore. We all know that some classes are great, and the students always do the right thing. We also know that there are some classes where you just want to pull your hair out—or theirs! But you can get things in order just by setting guidelines—and using them to refocus the group as needed.

Chances are that no matter what class you are teaching there will always be one! You know what I mean, the one that is a problem! The one that talks, the one that doesn't listen, the one who wants to be a smart aleck, the one who thinks he or she knows more than you do and of course, the one who just wants to make your life a misery! I am sure you have a few others that you can throw into that category. These students can really affect your classes, energy, creativity and flow. We have tried many techniques throughout the years and have found a few methods that produce good results.

I believe teachers must establish that they are in charge and that they will not tolerate any disrespect! You will need to show students that you mean business. It is not necessary to be a tyrant, but a firm and assured attitude is the key to keeping control. This can be demonstrated by what you say and by how you act. Students have to understand that if they misbehave, there will be consequences. If they are disrespectful or not behaving in class, give them at least one or two warnings. But if they persist, you may find it necessary to either have them sit down to watch the rest of the class or send them out of the room to demonstrate your point.

I like to focus on the one who is causing problems and try to get that person to be more mentally involved in the class. When there is a problem student, the natural reaction is to be annoyed at him or her. It is challenging to have a positive attitude when in reality you just want that person to go away! We don't enjoy teaching or having to deal with this type of student. Try to view it more as a challenge to win the student over. I know that can sometimes translate into a lot of hard work! Most of the time these kids are just screaming out for attention and don't care how they get it. Sometimes the ones who are struggling with the learning process just need a bit of one-on-one focus. Try to encourage the child to practice or take a private class with you. Talk to the parents and find out if there are problems at home or at school.

With the students who are having a hard time picking up a step, I will encourage them to practice at home. When they come back and show me that they have mastered the step and have practiced on their own, I make a big deal out of it. I let them lead the class in the step and then have their fellow students applaud their achievements. This can be highly contagious and will encourage others to follow suit!

Our goal as teachers is to challenge all of the students to learn and progress. Some will take the challenge faster and better than others. Some are born to dance. For the others, if we can teach them that practice and extra effort can result in advancement, then that will be a life lesson to enhance their lives more than any dance step!

You've got to have faith!

Believe in your corrections, believe in your teacher. Now repeat it again and again, and then write it down ten times. It should be a chant that all students older than the age of 8 say as they go into class!

Don't you love it when a student you teach comes to tell you about some revelation he or she just experienced in another class? It was a correction that you gave only 5,000 times! Finally the student gets it and hears it. Don't lose faith in yourself. You know what you are doing and that you are a good teacher. Students will learn, and you have the key.

It's all about the faith. No, I am not going to get religious on you now! It's about showing the students to trust you as a teacher and understand that you are there to guide them to a higher level. If they are there just for recreation, it is important to point out to them that part of recreation is to have fun.

In dance the real fun begins when you start to have a knowledge or vocabulary of steps. To master these steps, corrections will be given and, if applied, will lead to greater joy and self-expression. I like to use this analogy: If you have a piano and you sit down at it and play "chop sticks," how long will it take before you get bored with playing that? You need to learn, get better and broaden your knowledge.

The key is to inspire the students to have faith in what we are saying and know that, if they can understand the correction, they will get better.

So how do we do it?

How can we convince the students to have faith in what we say—and to love hearing any bit of information we impart to them?

How do we go beyond a correction, other than to verbalize, demonstrate and then have them do it?

Go that extra mile to show them that you care. I know that, in some ways, it may sound a bit corny. But we have found that it works like a charm every time. Students don't care about how much you know until they know how much you care, especially about them! Eye-to-eye contact and a smile will go a long way. Sometimes the most challenging students only want to know that someone really does care about them, even if the student has a funny way of asking for it. They are the ones who will really pull our focus and energy. The key is not to let them have it all. Sometimes just giving students a time out in class will do the trick. If students decide to be problematic for the day, I stop the class, make them go and sit down, and then watch the session. This sends a pretty strong message and usually is highly effective. No matter what happens, I always try to let students know in some way that I have their best interests in mind. I will not, however, let them get away with behavior that is detrimental to the rest of the class.

Receiving the gift of a correction!

That's right—it is a gift. I like to ask my students: When you receive a gift, do you make a face and push it away? Of course not! You smile and accept it with open arms! That is why we have our students **ALWAYS** say thank you for a correction. This sets the tone for accepting it in the manner it is given. It also allows the student to take ownership of the correction. I constantly tell my class that they are there to learn—recreational or not! I am there to teach, coach and give constructive criticism. By the way, we also have our students come up at the end of class to curtsey or bow, and say thank you for the class. It sets a tone of appreciation, and that is a good place to be in after any class.

Most parents just want their children to have fun, which means it is up to us to educate them and show them that we are teaching much more than dance. If students can learn to apply corrections toward solving a problem, how many times in their lives will that be used? It is building the right mindset for learning and promoting coping skills! Can I get a Halleluiah!

Bravo! Act Two Curtain Calls

Remember these things:

- Your success as a dance teacher begins and ends with you
- When it comes to teaching your classes, you are always in control and have the power to effect change if you so desire
- To inspire your students, you must stay inspired
- Getting a "Day Planner" is a great way to stay organized and on top of things
- It's important to take time for yourself and to always stay in balance
- While taking time off, try not to dwell on negative things
- Your students are a reflection of you
- If you expect a certain behavior from your students, they will follow your lead
- The best time to get control of your class is in the beginning of the year, by setting the tone with a list of guidelines, rules and regulations
- Give your students a print out of the rules to take home—it helps their parents understand that your classes are not a free-for-all nor are you a babysitting service
- If you have to reprimand students, always follow it up shortly after with a smile, so they know it is not personal
- Let them know before the class is over that you do not hold any grudges
- Establish that you are in charge and that you will not tolerate any disrespect
- Our goal as teachers is to challenge students to learn and progress

- Don't ever lose faith. Believe in yourself and know that you are a good teacher
- Always go the extra mile to show your students you care
- Remind your students that they are there to learn

Under the Stage Lights—Act Three: **Robert Landau**

> "Children have never been very good at listening to their elders, but they have never failed to imitate them."
>
> —*James Baldwin*

Ever demonstrate a routine and then wonder why students have issues catching on? What's the first thing you think when so many eyes look back at you with blank stares? The most common thing to do is internalize it. "Darn it, it's me—it's gotta be me. Something's off with my teaching style. My fault, I just know it's my fault!"

Would you consider that more often than not, it's something going on within your student and not you? All you can do is communicate. If you make a point of communicating in a clear and understandable manner, then you've done your part in sending your message. It's then up to your students to hear what you've said, internalize it and figure out how to give you back your suggestion. It's in this process that things tend to get a little stuck from time to time. Is it your fault? No. There's nothing wrong with things getting a little jumbled from time to time. That's what the teaching process is all about. You can't have teaching without learning. As you probably have come to realize, each student processes information differently. Each one of us absorbs and processes information in different ways.

Some students seem amazing. They hear you say something, watch you demonstrate it once, and then, before you can even finish what it is you are showing them, they mirror what you just modeled—to the letter. It's almost as if they didn't need even a moment to begin digesting what you modeled. They heard you, and now they are giving you back what you gave to them. Not all students learn in this way, though. Some need time to work out how they will show you that they've absorbed what you've taught them.

But what happens when nothing seems to move a class in a positive and productive direction? Consider examining the motivation. If students aren't feeling motivated, they aren't going to care about learning. That's all well and good, but how do you motivate students to benefit from what you have to offer, and empower them and get them excited about learning?

Here are four motivational teaching tips you might want to keep in mind as you move forward in your career:

Feel!

Many teachers can communicate effectively, but there's a difference between communicating and motivating. While it's true that you can't motivate unless you communicate, how you motivate can make a big difference. Think about injecting feeling into everything that you teach. Are you excited about what you are teaching? Do you stand behind it 100 percent, and just know that students will benefit if they follow your lead? Do your body language and voice mirror how you feel inside as you teach?

If you are really into what you teach, your students will feel it. Your enthusiasm will spread like wildfire. Enthusiasm, motivation and excitement are all energies that we send when we connect with our heart and fully believe what we are communicating. When was the last time you were truly excited about what you were teaching?

Always Acknowledge

Whether a routine is easy or difficult, always acknowledge and reward your students for jobs well done—and even for attempts that too often fall short of the mark. Sometimes praising those who make an honest effort has little to do with the outcome. Acknowledging a student's honest effort can often mean more to that person than can praise to those who find it easy to achieve. Either way, the important thing to remember is that positive feedback goes a long way in motivating students to take the next step. It's pretty rewarding for them to walk out of your class feeling as if they really accomplished something, especially if they walked in feeling like they couldn't do it. They'll keep coming back for more.

Have Fun!

Any level of perceived difficulty can be diminished if you approach it with fun in mind. Fun and humor can all but dissolve fear. You can get people to do something they once considered next to impossible—if they can approach the task with fun and lightheartedness. Suddenly, they understand how little there is to lose. Trying just might mean succeeding. Life is so much more worth living with healthy doses of fun along the way. It perks up energy, determination and spirit when there's a happy energy in the air.

You are the conductor of that orchestra, so to speak. If you lead with fun, others will follow in tandem. If you model a smile, others will pick it up and not even realize that they are mirroring the very same energy you show. Ever heard of the expression, "Time flies when you're having fun?" There's truth behind that cliché!

Get Involved

How much do you really care about what you do? Is your heart really in it? What's your level of commitment to the students you teach? How present are you when you teach classes? All of these go a long way in motivating students. What and how you really feel about things is a barometer for the outcome of the tasks you undertake. If you really aren't into what you are doing, the outcome will reflect it. It's the difference between a passing grade and an A+. Even if you put on a brave face and try to act like you care when you really don't, your students will register your true feelings on a certain level. It might not always be conscious, but you can be sure that they will pick up on it in some way, shape or form.

Being involved in teaching means being totally present. Involvement forces you to be there in the best way possible, and your students will feel lifted by your sense of commitment and care. Time flies when you are having fun, but it goes just as fast when you are totally present and involved with the task at hand.

Teaching should be your passion, or at least one of them. Passion connects directly with your heart. Heartfelt energy is infectious and can be a reason students tend to flock to those teachers who teach with their hearts. Teaching with your heart has everything to do with being involved. If you weren't involved with what you do, your heart wouldn't be such an important part of the mix.

Negativity Breeds Negativity!

Got any negative kids in your classes? What do you do about those guys, and is there any way to get them to come around?

First of all, see what happens when you apply these four tips. See how they work in motivating students of a negative nature. Watch for any kind of responses that might signal a shift to a more positive way of being. Small changes in a better direction are what are important here. Subtle shifts move mountains when it comes to transforming negative thinking. It might be worth it to chat with a student who seems more negative than the rest. Ask what, if anything, you can do to make this a better experience for that student. Show you care. One has to delicately dance around situations like this. Often, kids are dealing with extreme negative situations that exist elsewhere in their lives. They could be modeling this behavior by what they see and hear their parents doing. It could be something that's going on at school. Sometimes you don't even need to know. What you should focus on is making your class the absolute best part of your students' days with you. Asking what will help better the experience can show you are really there. If students feel safe with you and know you are one of the few who really care, they might feel comfortable showing you a side of them they never reveal to anyone else.

Conversely, it's also important to remember that you have things called boundaries. I believe there are two types of negative students. Those who might not even realize how negative they are due to the situations that seem to exist around them, and those who use negativity as a means of control to get what they want. Cater to the first group, and don't give an inch to the second!

Remember, though, that all you can do is the best that you can do—nothing more, but certainly nothing less. Negative students can be somewhat extreme in that their energy and attitudes end up disrupting the positive progress of the class. They can bring things down in a split second. If you've tried everything to shift a student's negative outlook but nothing seems to help, have a chat with your studio owner. See if he or she has any suggestions and try those. Keep a small written record of your efforts, including the day and dates that you tried them. This way, you demonstrate—through a backup and history—that you cared enough to remedy the situation.

If all else fails, you might have to talk to your studio owner about dismissing the student from your class simply because the student doesn't seem to be interested in being a student any longer. There's nothing wrong with parting ways if things don't work out. Maybe the student felt forced to take dance classes. With such a low interest in dance, maybe it's better if the child found another interest that resonates more.

As you can see, there are different levels of what it means to have a negative student in your class. As a teacher, I'm sure you realize that you wear many hats. In this particular case, one of them is that of a therapist. I'm not suggesting that you need to give counseling sessions, but I am saying that you need to discern what the level of negativity is for these students. Is that level low enough to work with and not have it harm the class progress, or is it high enough to truly block positive progress?

Negativity doesn't occur by accident. If you get negative students from time to time, there's a reason. You and the student need to learn from it, and then be sure to move on. You'll deal with the situation more effectively if you don't get stuck or freak out because you have negative students. With the negative messages all around us in society in this day and age it's no wonder students copy this behavior in their daily lives. You are one of the few who can stand out and show them what positive people and positive experiences look like. Put on your leadership hat and be an example of positivity in their lives. Let your class be a shining light in a student's life of relative darkness and that person will remember and thank you forevermore.

Bravo! Act Three Curtain Calls

Remember these things:

- If you make a point of communicating in a clear and understandable manner, then you've done your part in conveying your message
- Teaching doesn't happen without learning
- If students aren't motivated, they won't care about learning
- Inject feeling and excitement into everything that you teach
- Your body and voice should mirror your excitement and commitment to teaching
- Always acknowledge and reward your students for jobs well done, and for attempts that often fall short of the mark
- Put fun into everything you do
- Teaching with your heart has everything to do with being involved
- Subtle shifts move mountains when it comes to transforming negative thinking
- Focus on making your class the best part of your student's day
- All you can do is the very best you can do!
- You are one of the few who can stand out and show your students what a positive person and a positive experience look like
- Let your class be a shining light in a student's life of relative darkness

NOTES

Looking for more inspiration?
Get your FREE copy of the Dance Teacher Web
Monthly Newsletter every month at
www.danceteacherweb.com

D'Valda & Sirico Dance and Music Centre

Chapter 5

In Front of the Proscenium

In Front of the Proscenium—Act One: **Angela D'Valda Sirico**

> "Keep steadily before you the fact that all true success depends at last upon yourself."
>
> —*Theodore T. Hunger*

When you attend a performance the first thing that you notice about the performers is the way they present themselves to you. It is only after checking out their appearance—the way they are dressed and the type of attitude exhibited—that you will go to the next step of assessing talent. Why is it that the first impression people have of you determines how they view you as a professional?

When you, as a teacher, go for a job interview, that first appearance will be extremely important. When you show up to teach a class, you will be judged on your appearance by students and parents. Why does that happen? It is chiseled into our culture. Experts say we normally take only a very few seconds to decide what kind of a person is standing in front of us. Of course, many a first impression gives a wrong impression, but unfortunately, good or bad, that first impression tends to stick in our minds. Teachers, and especially dance teachers, must not only make a good first impression, but they have to keep making that good impression, day in and day out, for all of their audiences. So how can you be sure to achieve a great first impression? You can certainly start with a checklist of important features. Here are my favorite eleven items:

***Be on Time**
***Be Confident**
***Be Yourself**
***Be Positive**
***Be Presentable**
***Be Eager**
***Be Polite**
***Be Interested**
***Be Interesting**
***Be Smart**
***Be Nurturing**

If you can bring any or all of these features to the table, you will definitely have an extremely good shot at giving a great impression.

"If we teach today as we taught yesterday, we rob our students of tomorrow."
—John Dewey

Be On Time

Being punctual and ready to teach is important and keeps you constantly employed. At my studio, if a teacher has been constantly late or arrives exactly when the class is supposed to start, it is a problem. It shows employers that you are not professional or don't consider it important to be there and ready to greet your students. To be on top of the job, you really do need to arrive at least fifteen minutes before your first class starts. Of course there can be extenuating circumstances and any organization will understand that. It is only when it becomes a regular pattern that the red flag goes up. Personally, I hate the feeling of having to rush in at the last moment, and when this has happened to me, I have managed to make it work for my students. But I feel greatly uncomfortable in myself.

Be Confident

Confidence usually builds with experience and knowledge. If teachers lack confidence, you will tell by the way they structure their classes, by the tone of their voices and by the way they approach their students. Of course, the more knowledge teachers have, the more they feel that they have to give to their students. But it will also mean that they have more to give to their employers. That is why it is vitally important to keep training both the mind and the body. It can be hard to find the time for continuing education—we are usually pretty busy people—but the benefits of continuing to learn far out way the negatives. First of all, we live in an ever changing dance world. To stay current with new techniques and approaches to teaching, we need to study them. Not doing so makes it easy to get left in the dust. But more importantly, we need to stay motivated and help our students stay that way, too. That was our primary reason for creating Dance Teacher Web—to give all dance teachers a chance to stay current and keep them motivated on a daily basis. Of course it helps to build into your yearly schedule the times when you can attend teacher training sessions. These are times with no students, when you can spend quality time just developing yourself without distractions.

When you have confidence in yourself as a teacher, it can help you negotiate with your employer for a good salary and good terms in your contract. Most employers will take note when they feel that you would be an asset to their companies and will be much more ready to give you the price that you request. The tone of your voice, though, can be a sure sign of lack of confidence in a teacher. We once hired a teacher who was very knowledgeable and a good person. Her only downfall was that, when she taught, she sounded as though she was screeching at the students and they absolutely hated it. She was just not getting the results or connection with her students. I suggested at the time that she work with a voice coach to find another way to project her voice since she was so valuable in all other ways. She actually did do that, and as a result has stayed employed and grown to be a favorite teacher with the students. Just that one small adjustment in her delivery made her a much more usable teacher.

Be Yourself

Sometimes teachers are afraid to be themselves. Yet your personality can make the difference between being an "OK" teacher and an excellent one. This ties in with being confident, but as long as you bring an upbeat personality to the table, it will really work for you. Your employer wants to know your personality, and your students will gravitate to you when you let them see you as a human being! At the end of the day, you want to have fun, enjoy going to work and happily interact with the people you deal with daily. On those days when you just are not feeling it, you will be grateful for the acting ability dance taught you. It will help present your personality to all in a positive light.

Be Positive

Certainly, we see enough negativity in the world—if we can teach in a positive manner, it will help eradicate some of those vibes. Corrections in class are a must, and it can truly drive you crazy when students keep making the same mistakes. But keeping corrections positive will bring better results. Motivating students to practice and fix their mistakes is part of our challenge. I always tell my students that repeating mistakes calls for a new approach that will wake up their brains and help find a way to fix the mistakes. Keeping our thoughts positive can challenge us, and times or circumstances can get in the way of positive thoughts. But teachers who always complain or moan about how bad everything is can be depressing and will alienate colleagues—and employers. We all have our burdens to bear, but there really is a time and place to do that. At work is not a good place. If there is an occasional issue, I'm sure everyone would be supportive and help find positive solutions.

Be Presentable

How you present yourself matters. People really do judge others by their appearance, rightly or wrongly so. How you come to work, what you wear to teach and even how you come dressed to performances is important. Again, it is all a measure of how professional you are. If a teacher looks disheveled in class, it is not a good message to send to students, parents or employer. How can students be expected to come to class wearing the right attire if a teacher doesn't seem to care? What's appropriate depends upon the kind of classes you teach, but being well groomed is a must. Some employers will tell you exactly what to wear for classes and others will leave it up to your discretion. Then it is up to you to make the right choices.

Be Eager

How easy it can be to lose that eagerness we have for a new job or project. At first, we are enormously enthusiastic, which can be contagious! It usually results in everyone around us getting fired up, too. The key is to keep that great feeling all year by finding ways to ignite it in each class we teach. You lead by example, and others will find it easy to follow if you project that image. It is not always easy to be eager, but if you take a moment each day to think about how to generate that excitement for yourself and others around you, it will get results. Sometimes you need only to look at something a different way to get that enthusiasm going. Your employer will appreciate the energy and eagerness you bring to your classes and it will certainly generate new ideas helpful to you and the studio or school.

Be Polite

This seems like such a basic practice, but unfortunately in this day and age, it is becoming a lost art! It really comes down to respect for one another. Simple acts like saying "hello" when you enter the studio or showing genuine interest in how others feel, show respect. At our studio, we teach our students to say hello when they come in and to stop talking when a teacher enters the room. We ask them to thank the teacher for any correction, as they would for any gift they receive, and to curtsey and bow individually to the teacher at the end of each class. I like to thank the students for coming to class and for trying their hardest. Sometimes in our busy lives we can all forget about the basic manners that are so important to keeping good relationships going. Again, if we want our students to follow us in a positive way, then we need to set the right example.

Be Interested

Finding ways to be interested in others will make your relationships better and more fun. So often we become wrapped up in our own day-to-day events that we don't take the time to listen to the people in our lives, or be interested in what is happening to them.

Perhaps at work you run in to teach your classes without ever stopping to see what is going on around you. It is so easy for that to happen, yet if we set aside extra time to talk with the people we encounter in our worlds, how enriching that would be.

Why not suggest to your employer how the classes or the school can be improved? As a studio owner, I really appreciate it when any of my teachers offer new ideas. No one person can think of everything and it shows me that the teachers are truly invested in our program. There is a powerful camaraderie that forms when you are a team and it can bring long-term employment and friendships. At the end of the day, everyone wants to feel noticed and important, and our success and happiness depend upon the way we relate to others.

Be Interesting

Are you the type of person who is upbeat and positive or do you tend to bring your problems to work and to your friends? Of course, we all have moments when a problem must be presented and laid on the table in the hope that our co-workers or friends can help us solve it. We will, however, be considered far more interesting if that happens less frequently. The more we can bring positive moments to the people around us, the more interested in us they will be. Our life's experiences, good and bad, can help someone else along the way. If we can keep people's interest in what we do and say, we will gain tremendous respect and friendships. Generally it follows that if you are interesting; it is because you are interested.

Be Smart

Staying professional is always important when you are a teacher. It can be very tempting in this day and age for teachers to "friend" their students on Facebook or contact them through other social media. This is more prevalent with younger teachers because they have been brought up in the media age. I cannot emphasize enough how big of a mistake it is to let your students view your personal Facebook page or to let them "friend" you. Do you really want them to know every detail of your personal life? A professional Facebook page is different, one devoted to your teaching, choreography and perhaps student achievements. But once you cross that very thin line between professional and personal, it can lead to a multitude of problems from your employer, your students and their parents. As dance teachers we do become close to some of our students. But it is important for all to maintain our dignity and keep the respect we earn each day. It is always safer to not become friends with the parents of your students, something that can lead to problems with the perceptions of others.

Be Nurturing

The way teachers connect with their students is truly the key to success. In almost every class we teach, there are discrepancies between students and their levels of talent. But each one of those students has the need to be recognized in some way by the teacher. A simple use of eye contact or an encouraging smile can be all it takes to keep a student happy and eager to work for you. It is a good idea to make a comment to each dancer at some moment in the class. It could be asking how he or she is feeling or having that student step forward to demonstrate something done well or improved upon. Do anything you can to spotlight that person, even for a short moment, and validate that he or she exists and is important to you. Young students are very often lacking in confidence, and this validation will help them build themselves up in a positive way—and will be something they remember for a lifetime. Some students get very upset when given corrections and feel they are being "picked on." For those individuals, it is always a good idea to finish the class with some kind of uplifting or humorous word to keep their spirits up.

Bravo! Act One Curtain Calls

Remember these things:

- First impressions are lasting impressions
- To be on top of the job, you really do need to arrive at least fifteen minutes before your first class starts
- When you have confidence in yourself as a teacher, it lets you negotiate with your employer
- The tone of your voice can signal a lack of confidence from a teacher
- Your personality makes the difference between being an "OK" teacher and being a really excellent one
- Always bring an upbeat personality to the table
- There is enough negativity in the world; if we can teach in a positive manner, it will help to eradicate some of those vibes
- Teachers who always complain about how bad everything is will alienate other teachers and employers
- The way in which you choose to present yourself makes a huge difference
- Find ways to ignite eagerness into every class you teach
- Saying hello when you enter the studio or showing genuine interest in how someone else is feeling fosters relationships
- Be interested and interesting!
- Keep your personal life separate from your teaching life

In Front of the Proscenium—Act Two: **Steve Sirico**

"Don't limit yourself. Many people limit themselves to what they think they can do. You can go as far as your mind lets you. What you believe, you can achieve."
—Mary Kay Ash

I would like for you to think about the people you really admire. Think about what they do or how they carry themselves. Here are some questions I would like for you to consider:

- What is it about them that sticks out?
- What makes them special in your eyes?
- Now, think about how they present themselves.

I recommend you take notice of how they behave and interact with other people. Now think about how you are viewed by those around you. How you interact, dress, groom yourself and speak all go into how others perceive you.

Studies show that it takes only seven seconds to make an impression—good or bad! That's right—the length of time it took you to read that last line is all it takes to plant an impression in another person's mind about you.

Remember it all starts the minute you enter the studio.

- Many eyes are on you, so I would like for you to consider:
- How do you walk in to the studio?
- Are you friendly?
- Do you make eye contact with the people you pass?
- Do you make a point of saying hi?
- How are you dressed?

Here are fourteen ways to make a good impression!

The impression you give to your class, and your employer, will be a big factor in the treatment you receive back from them. Your success in what you do will have a direct correlation between your image and the attitude image you project. It has been said that the world around you is like a mirror. The way you react will be the way others react to you. Let's face it, how many unhappy people do you know who are surrounded by happy people? How many successful, eager, up-and-coming people do you know who hang around with those who appear to be losers? If you want to change your surroundings, it may be best to start by making a few changes to your image. It is important to get off to a good start and best of all, you hold the key. However, you may need to clean things up. Don't distress—if you make a few changes, people will notice and you will notice a BIG difference in how they treat you! The tips below will apply to your classroom, meeting new people in a social setting and making a good impression with an employer.

Here are tips to make a great impression!

1. Own the room. When you enter the building, stand tall and walk in with confidence.
2. Smile. You'll appear more approachable and confident.
3. Be the first to reach out. Extend your hand and give a firm handshake when meeting a parent or applying for a job. A weak handshake is an immediate turnoff.
4. Look directly into someone's eyes. Do not scan the room while talking to one person. This is especially important when you are giving a correction to a student or meeting a parent for the first time.
5. Don't chew gum when you enter the building.
6. Speak clearly and pause. Sloppy or hurried speech is perceived as negative. Eliminate slang.
7. Be fully present. Focus on the person and listen non-verbally, using body language.
8. Ask questions about them instead of talking about yourself.
9. Find common ground quickly. This will build instant rapport.
10. Give compliments. Your students will respond better to

corrections, your employer will appreciate that you notice positive changes, and parents will love that you care!

11. Paraphrase. It's a form of acknowledging people. This skill makes you very attractive. It communicates that you are listening.
12. Have something interesting to say. Comment on the other person's interests.
13. Be a giver. Offer a tip or an introduction to others. Give without expecting anything in return.
14. Mirror the other person. Match their speaking rate, volume level, and words. If they speak fast, quicken your pace. If they are soft-spoken, lower your volume. People like people who are most like them.

Always Remember: It takes 7 seconds or less to make a good first impression. You're always on stage.

Ok, you may be thinking, wow Steve; this is a lot of work. If people don't like me for who I am, then too bad for them. Well, if you want to succeed in life, then you need to adjust that way of thinking. The reality of the world is that it really isn't all about you. Most people only care about themselves. So if you can leave your ego at the door and make others feel important, you will be a success in life. Read that line a few times because if you get nothing else out of this part of my chapter then you will be way ahead of the game and will excel in all you do!

Are you happy where you are today? If the answer is yes, then keep up the good work and keep looking for ways to make it even better! If the answer is no then the good news is you can create change if you believe you can do it. If you want to differentiate yourself from everyone else, then you need to be different in some ways from everyone else.

Looking to stand out in the crowd? Consider these questions.

In The Classroom:

- Do your students think of you as a disciplinarian?
- Do your students think you are an easygoing individual?

- Do they respect you?
- When you mean business, do they listen carefully?
- Do you complain to them about your life or work issues?
- Do you let your students, even the problem ones, get under your skin?
- Do you connect with them outside the studio on a personal level?
- Do you know how to draw the line between teacher and friend?

With Your Employer:

- Do you communicate with the studio owner effectively?
- Do you like to please your boss and refrain from confrontation?
- Are you honest with your employer in regards to your view of the school and how you can all make it better?
- Are you comfortable asking for a raise?
- Do you present ideas that will improve your classes and the students experience in your class?
- Do you like who you work for?

Some of these questions may even make you feel a bit uncomfortable, and if they do, good! Look, if you want to keep improving and developing yourself as a teacher, then you need to take a hard look at how you do things. Your answers may even surprise you. If you find you do not like your answers or if you find they may be part of your problem, the good news is that you can most definitely change what you do. Relationships are ever evolving, and a new outlook by you will translate to others and that will be contagious.

When You Have The Right Mindset So Will Your Students!

As any teacher will testify, it is ultimately all about the students. You will be judged on how much they have learned, how well they have performed their dance, and whether their piece of choreography was entertaining. I always believe that students are a reflection of their teacher. If they don't look good, the teacher doesn't look good! Getting your students to learn and to look good starts with them having the right mindset, which in turn, will help them to exceed their goals! This may seem simple enough but is not easy when a class or student has a poor attitude. Your joy, love and energy can be contagious. We want all of our students to have a positive mindset when it comes to learning. Especially for example, when they are having an issue with a step or combination. Making them understand that working hard on something to get it right very often ends with a positive result and is therefore worth the effort. This is important.

Sometimes students don't really believe they can do certain things because they doubt their own capabilities. When you have a good student who starts to give you an attitude, it is important to find out why. Students who do this are probably thinking that they know it all and of course, at that point, simply stop learning. We have found that by talking to them and trying to help them focus on why they started dancing in the first place, we can often reignite their desire to learn. A lot of the time, trouble starts with these students because their parents are filling their heads with over-inflated ideas. So it is a good idea to sit down and discuss what is happening before the situation gets out of control. If you can instill early in the students that the right mindset in their approach to work fosters their success, then you have helped them tremendously.

Here Are Some Ideas To Focus On:

- I do not allow our students to say "I can't do that" or any other phrase that starts with "I can't." They can say "I am having trouble, can you help me?" or "That step is difficult for me, what can I do to improve?"
- A correction is a gift. After a correction, I have the students say thank you as a sign of appreciation to the teacher for seeing something in them that can be improved. When I find that students are not responding to their corrections, I have a quick talk after class—just to let them know that I expect more out of them. There are no hard feelings. I simply need for them to work harder to reach their full potential.
- Tune in to learning. Once students reach a certain level, they must

fine-tune their corrections. This part of the training will be up to the student. To fix those little technical flaws will take focus and persistence, and will not be easy. But it will be very rewarding and empowering when finished.

- No folded arms. This comes from the old saying, "Closed arms, closed mind." I couldn't agree more! I tell the students to stand tall, shoulders back, chin lifted and arms relaxed by their sides.
- Keep smiling! I want to see happy faces, and I want them to have fun. Joyous and happy feelings create a good environment for learning. I want our students to respect us not fear us. How great is it when you teach a class, and students are pumped up and uplifted as they leave. Make this a goal on how to end each and every class!

Smiling and having a genuine feeling of thankfulness will translate into all you do. Keep in mind that you are always on stage. Your work is being evaluated and so is how you act, dress and interact with others. Make sure you are projecting the kind of reputation you want.

> "Every time you smile at someone, it is an action of love, a gift to that person, a beautiful thing."
>
> —*Unknown, but often attributed to Mother Teresa*

Bravo! Act Two Curtain Calls

Remember these things:

- It takes only seven seconds to make an impression, good or bad
- The impression you give to your class and your employer will be a big factor in the treatment you will receive back from them
- Your success in what you do you will have a direct correlation between your image and the attitude image you project
- Always remember to smile. It sets the tone of confidence and makes you much more approachable
- If you can leave your ego at the door and make others feel important, you will be a success in life
- If you have the right mindset, so will your students
- Students are always a reflection of their teacher
- Instill in your students that having the right mindset in their approach to work builds success
- Don't allow your students to say "I can't"
- A correction is a gift
- Folded or closed arms = a closed mind
- Smiling and having a genuine feeling of thankfulness will translate into all you do

In Front of the Proscenium—Act Three: **Robert Landau**

> "I don't want to be perfect, but I do want to be a role model. My mom always tells me that imperfections equal beauty. All of us are imperfect."
>
> —*Miley Cyrus*

Not too long ago, I heard someone say, "Hey, a teacher is a teacher is a teacher—nothing more, nothing less!" How does that statement make you feel? You might have a somewhat negative reaction to these words. If that's the case, what is it about this statement that makes you feel that way?

From the outside looking in, many people who don't have any teaching experience have no idea what's required of a teacher nowadays. They have little to no idea of what it is like to be in your shoes. You can't blame them really, but realizing this one simple fact might help you understand where people are coming from when they don't react to situations the way you had hoped.

To be an effective, memorable and efficient dance teacher today, you have to be up on all the latest developments concerning your craft. You need to be a positive role model, you have to have copious amounts of patience, and if that isn't enough, you should always have a smile plastered on your face—even when that's the last thing you feel like doing. You likewise must be professional at all times and have what it takes to weather any storm. Is this you? If you don't think you have all of these traits and even more, think again. Let's look at this another way. On a scale of one to ten, ten being "Absolutely Amazing!" and one being the polar opposite, how would you rate yourself as a teacher? All I ask is that you think carefully and be fair with yourself in how you respond to this question.

So what did you come up with? If you didn't respond with a ten, I truly understand. But I would also ask you to consider the possibility that you might be selling yourself short. Why? I believe all teachers have a perfect ten within them. Ten is 100 percent of your potential as a teacher. When you are a ten, you are at the top of your game. You are unique, and people tend to take notice of you. There's a certain buzz about who you are and what you do.

If you answered seven or eight, no problem! There really isn't a right or wrong way to answer this question. If you did respond with a seven or eight, it could be that you are only realizing 70 or 80 percent of your true potential. As a teacher, you always have a true 100 percent potential within you. The question is do you believe this is so? If you don't then, you might be preventing yourself from being all you can be as a teacher—and as a fully realized person.

Do you believe you have everything it takes to be a truly great dance teacher? When it comes to the subject of you, I do! How could I possibly believe something like this? Because anyone who wants to be a teacher wants to be the best teacher possible. If your heart's in it, then it would stand to reason you wouldn't settle for anything less. You wouldn't have decided to teach if you didn't think you could do it. Think about it. Airline pilots wouldn't choose that field if they didn't think they could fly a plane, right? Somewhere, someplace within you, you have the potential to be everything you want to be. In many ways, you are already there. You just need to remember what you might have forgotten and in so doing, prove to yourself that you have what it takes to truly succeed as a dance instructor.

You probably can conclude that I truly believe each and every one of us came here with 100 percent potential. That's how most of us were born, and that's also how we should have maintained ourselves as we continued on our life's journey. A bird is born with the potential to fly. It's part of being a bird. It's in the learning to fly that we connect with our potential within. No one comes along and tells the bird it can't fly. That instinct and knowing lies within every cell of its body. Flying becomes the bird's destiny.

Most of us have let numerous outside influences convince us that we aren't all we thought we could be. Family members, friends, peers, the media and so many more—we gave these entities the power to tell us who we are and what we're truly capable of, rather than simply listening to our heart and following its lead.

Are there things as a teacher you feel you might lack? Sure! It's only natural to feel that way. None of us is perfect all the time. Feelings of doubt or lack shouldn't be looked at as a negative. These are things that can all be added and integrated into the mix as time moves on. That's part of our learning experience and the journey of life. Say you don't feel you have the patience required to keep things positive in class from time to time. There's nothing wrong with feeling this way. Maybe this is something you need to work on. But it's how you think and feel about this issue that makes all the difference in the world. Because you have a seeming lack of something, is this a negative? Not really. It's just something you need to address. It's not like you never had patience in your life. In this instance, through various situations that have occurred, you just forgot you had it.

Addressing an issue such as this is neither negative nor positive. It just needs to be addressed. All too often we tend to assign something like this as a negative and then to make matters even worse, we proceed to brow-beat ourselves into the ground because we think something is wrong and it makes us imperfect. As I said before, most of us were born perfect, but we've forgotten our original state of perfection as time marched on. So in the case of one's lack of patience when it comes to the classroom, you just need to remember what having patience is like and then integrate that feeling into your daily existence. If you don't have much patience in class with students, it might follow that you don't have much patience with certain things in your life. Is this a bad thing? Only if you think it is. Don't attach judgment to this issue and do what it takes to be more patient. Problem solved!

You have everything you need to succeed as a teacher. All you have to do is believe and feel that this is indeed the case—and then walk it and talk it. Even though we aren't always perfect, there is perfection in our incompleteness. Knowing you are doing the absolute best you can means that you are being the absolute best you can be. No one can ask more of you than that, including you yourself.

As you move from day to day, always remember that as a teacher, you are a role model. This doesn't only apply to the students who are lucky enough to be with you on your journey. It also includes other staff members in your workplace. It's a good idea to break away from the old adage that tells employees to treat co-workers differently than the customers they all serve. Everyone is in the same boat. We're all human beings working toward the same goal—to have a bit of fun and get a bit of joy and meaning out of the short time we are here. The better we treat one another, and the more kindness and respect we model as part of our being, the better off our workplace will be and the world as a whole. If you show respect for yourself as a person, then it only stands to reason you would have the same for the students you teach. It also makes sense that you would have the same respect you show to yourself and to your students, to other faculty members and yes, even to parents! When situations arise, as they always will, work through them step by step, all the while believing a satisfactory conclusion will be reached and accepted by all. There's a reason why you decided to become a dance teacher. Each day holds valuable lessons on what it means to teach. Take these lessons and grow. You are being taught as you teach.

Here are some interesting questions for you to ponder. They will help shape you as a teacher and get you back in touch with why you might have decided to become a dance teacher in the first place. Being honest with how you answer these questions will help you focus on the many rewards and benefits of doing what you do. I will not attempt to answer these questions for you because that's something only you can do. My comments can be useful tools to help you arrive at worthwhile conclusions. Ready?

Would you say that you are a 'gift' to your students, and if so, how?

In all you say and do, realize that you are a walking, talking role model who has the power to change young lives for the better. The smallest difference you make can go the farthest when it comes to creating change. We've all had a teacher we'll never forget. Why can't that be you? It's what you bring to the table that makes all the difference in the world. It's YOUR difference and no one else's. Wondering how to make a difference? Lead and teach from your heart, not your mind.

What are some of the things your students can take away from your classes that go into making them better people?

This has a lot to do with being a role model. Your enthusiasm and love for what you do ends up being a part of your unique energy, style and overall class experience. It's something unique to you. Empower your students and they will give you back tenfold the goodness and caring you gave to them.

If you are indeed a role model, what you would say you are a role model for?

Who and how you see yourself as a teacher shapes the vibe you give off that others will follow. What vibe are you giving off that others notice? All of this has to do with being a leader, which is another way of saying role model, which in effect is another way of saying teacher.

What's special and unique about you?

The message should be clear by now. You never need to be something you aren't as a teacher. Do what feels right to you. Make things engaging and fun.

What's the one thing you have that no other teacher in the dance studio world has?

Only you can know this for sure. I can only assume it has to do with energy uniquely yours and yours alone. What your students love and admire about you ends up being your unique "medicine." It's a potion whose special ingredients no one else has but you. As varied and different as all of us are, there is only one you.

Why did you decide to become a dance teacher, and do you feel that you are still being true to your original reason for getting into this industry?

Even if you don't think your reason for being a teacher is still present, consider that it always has been. It might be you've temporarily lost touch with the reason. If that's the case, all you have to do it reconnect with your original intention. It's there. All you have to do is breathe, relax and find it once again.

Where do you see yourself five years from now?

Do you see yourself in the industry? Committing yourself to grow and learn is something that happens on a daily basis. If you keep things moving in a positive direction as time moves on, you'll be in such a wonderful place five years into the future that you won't even know what to do with yourself. Setting your intention on being the best you can be in your chosen profession means that all kinds of amazing things will make themselves known to you as time marches on. All you have to do is be open to the wonder of it all. As with everything in life, it's a choice. You always stand at the door. Do you leave it open or choose to keep it shut?

There are many who believe that nothing happens by accident. If you resonate with this type of idea, then your being a dance teacher was truly meant to be. Knowing this is only part of the equation though. The other half has everything to do with keeping yourself on a positive course as time goes on and being open to change. See yourself where you want to be in the future right here and now, and watch what happens. Want to be the best you can be? Then realize that you have everything you need to get there already residing deep within you. Ride on the crest of the wave of your profession and what it is to be a dance teacher and it will be everything you want it to be—and more.

Bravo! Act Three Curtain Calls

Remember these things:

- All teachers have a perfect ten within them
- Somewhere, someplace within, you have the potential to be everything you want to be
- You have everything you need to succeed as a teacher. All you have to do is believe and feel that this is indeed the case and then walk it and talk it
- Even though we aren't always perfect, there is perfection in our incompleteness
- Knowing you are doing the absolute best you can means you are being the absolute best you can be
- Always remember that as a teacher, you are a role model
- Each day holds valuable lessons as to what it means to teach. Take these lessons and grow
- The smallest difference you make can go the farthest when it comes to creating change
- Lead and teach from your heart, not your mind
- What your students love and admire about you ends up being your unique "medicine"
- Committing yourself to grow and learn is something that happens on a daily basis
- Your being a dance teacher was truly meant to be
- See where you want to be in your future in the here and now. Then always work toward that goal

NOTES

STARRING . . . YOU!!!

Chapter 6

How to Get Your Name in Lights

How to Get Your Name in Lights—Act One: **Angela D'Valda Sirico**

> "What lies behind us and what lies before us are small matters compared to what lies within us."
>
> —*Ralph Waldo Emerson*

The reason you became a dance teacher comes from your past. The reality that you currently are a dance teacher is in the present. And where you go from here is totally up to you. Sometimes dance teachers do not think of themselves as a product or business, yet that is what we are. How we promote ourselves or our business is going to be the deciding factor in how high up the ladder of success we can go.

First and foremost you need to decide if you are happy where you are now. If you are not, then it is definitely time to start promoting yourself and investigating where and what would be the best fit for you. If you are happy, now is the time to look closely at yourself and your worth professionally to see how much farther you can go. Some teachers are employees and work for the school systems, colleges and dance studios. Some are independent contractors and travel all over the country and possibly the world to teach their classes at studios, conferences and conventions. Some focus on the occasional class but mostly do choreography. Whatever type of teacher you are or want to become, you will absolutely benefit from marketing yourself whenever possible.

Once you have decided which avenue you want to take, then you can begin to get yourself organized. Make a list of all your good qualities, as a professional and in your personal life. Do you have an outgoing personality, or are you the quiet and shy type? What makes you and your classes unique? Perhaps you are the only teacher in your area qualified and certified to teach the Royal Academy of Dance Syllabus, the Cecchetti system or American Ballet Theatre's children's syllabus. Maybe you yourself studied with a master teacher in jazz or tap or modern and have added your own touches that you want to pass on to students. Is choreography one of your strengths? Whatever you can bring to the table that sets you apart from other teachers in your area—use it to promote who you are as a teacher. That is why the more you know about your craft the better. Investing time and money into becoming a better teacher will most certainly pay off in the future. The more knowledge you can acquire and the more experience you have, the more valuable you become to any employer.

Joining a teacher community can be extremely beneficial because it gives you the opportunity to network with other teachers. It also gives you more options to become a better teacher. When you can talk to other dance teachers from around the world, it opens your eyes to the fact that we are all identical, with the same problems and the same pressures. But it also could give you an opportunity to travel and teach that you probably would not have had otherwise. I know of dance teachers who have been asked to fly to the other side of the globe to teach at a dance school, after they met and talked with teachers at a conference. On the whole, dance teachers do not communicate with each other that much. But why not share experiences with one another?—especially when by doing so, it can open up doors to some interesting work.

The importance of marketing yourself

Just because you work at a local studio doesn't mean you cannot market yourself to other organizations. In the beginning, focus on what you can realistically achieve but do not limit yourself to the present. Envision where you want to be this time next year and then five years from now, because if you don't it will be very easy to become stuck in the "now"—and that could lead to becoming very stagnant and lacking in inspiration. Trust yourself, trust your knowledge and trust your ability to teach. Then start to make some moves.

I suggest every dance teacher invest in printing professional cards. Include a description of what you do and all of your contact information.

These should be given out at any opportunity—when networking or even when meeting people for the first time. Most professional people carry their cards with them as a way to get their name out. You might think to yourself, "Where am I going to go or who am I going to meet who would be interested in receiving my card?" Well, you would be surprised. You never know who knows whom, and many a position has been offered by someone receiving a business card. It is the professional thing to do, and unfortunately too many dance teachers do not see themselves as part of the professional work force. Of course we love what we do, but so do doctors and lawyers and financial advisors. If we are to be treated the way we should be, after all the years of study we have put into our trade, then we must carry ourselves with the same authority.

Make decisions on where and what you want to teach

Deciding where you want to teach is an important decision. Depending on what qualifications you possess, you may want to apply to a college or university with a dance program. The school systems also need dance teachers because many of the "dance" teachers in the school systems are really physical education teachers with a limited knowledge of dance. The majority of dance teachers work in dance schools or studios. There is always a need for good teachers, and the chance of long-term employment is good, as long as you enjoy working with children of all ages and can constantly bring new ideas to keep the students stimulated. If your students are happy and your employer is happy with you, it will help you keep your position at the school and can open the door for a possible raise. You do need to have a passion for teaching, because if you are only teaching for the paycheck and not really interested in the students, that will soon be noticed. It could eventually result with the termination of your job.

You may want to teach at conventions and conferences, and in that case, you need to send your resume to the organizations that interest you. Many dance conventions also have a competition attached to them, in which case you will almost always be required to judge the competition. For this type of job, it is an asset if you have danced professionally. The employer wants to publicize your professional achievements to make the classes look more attractive. You definitely need to be good at crowd control for these classes—it is not uncommon to have a hundred or more students in any given class.

It is a good idea to get yourself signed with an agent who represents dance teachers working on that circuit. You will find those mostly in the biggest cities of whichever country you live in. All agents receive a commission for finding you the work, but will typically invoice the employer separately or put it on top of the amount you want to receive.

Next you need to decide what you would like to be paid for your classes. The way to approach this is to find out what other teachers with the same amount of experience are receiving in your area. Where you live will be a deciding factor as far as wages go. Amount of experience will almost certainly be taken into consideration as will any special talents you bring to the table. This can be a unique type of class you teach or a foreign language you speak or professional teacher certification. Obviously you need to be fair and realistic about the amount you want. Most employers will do their best to give you an amount both you and they can live with. It is usually dependent on how much money is coming into the business and how much can reasonably be allocated for wages. Once you have discovered what the going rate is, use it. When going for an interview with a prospective employer, ask for the higher end of the spectrum. If the person interviewing you feels it is above what the studio can pay you, then he or she will negotiate with you until you are both satisfied. It is, however, pointless to inflate your price beyond reason. Another factor that will come into play is whether or not you feel a good connection at the school or studio, because without that, the money really doesn't matter. Nine times out of ten, it will not work out to a happy ending.

Whatever type of situation you seek, make sure you are extremely well prepared. Create the right image for yourself through promotional materials, and the way you dress and act. All of these are important as you move forward and project to your employer, students and their parents that you are a professional.

As far as promotional materials go, I have already talked about the value of business cards. But there are other ways to promote what you do and what you create. Make up a flyer that is colorful and eye catching that describes your classes. If you find the design end of it difficult, find someone who can design it for you at a reasonable price. You could add a coupon or some sort of call to action that will encourage anyone looking at the flyer to try out your classes. Make a professional webpage that shows short, edited versions of the type of choreography you produce or a video of your class. You don't need to show anything very long as people nowadays are busy and their attention span is short. Make it easy for them to want to contact you, but make sure it is through the right avenues and not through a personal Facebook page. There have been occasions when teachers have been dismissed for becoming too friendly with students or clients. There is absolutely a line that should not be crossed if you want to maintain your professional status. There are also websites where you can advertise as a dance teacher if you are looking for employment. You can find these sites by doing a Google search. Setting up a blog is another effective way to let people in the industry become aware of what you are doing professionally. Using one method to market you and your business generally does not work; it is by combining different ways that you can achieve the best end result.

Reliability is key!

I cannot stress enough the importance of being reliable when you are working as a teacher—or really when you are working anywhere. Your employer needs to know that he or she can count on you to be where you should be when you are supposed to be there. There are times when a sudden illness or a transportation issue makes it hard to get to your job. But a phone call is needed to give your employer time to deal with the situation and to make sure the classes run as smoothly as possible with little or no interruption for clients. This is a common courtesy but one that is sometimes forgotten. You **are** your business, and you are the CEO and faculty of your business. So it is extremely important that you do not develop a reputation for being unreliable—that will have a negative effect on you and your business. The dance world is pretty small, and it doesn't take long for the word to spread, whether it is good or bad. You need to establish your good name and then protect it, because you have probably put in a lot of time and effort and money to get where you are.

Dance teachers are called upon constantly to come up with creative ideas for performances that occur during any given year. What do you do to keep those ideas flowing? Most instructors have their own ways of coming up with choreography. It is generally much easier to do that with our most-advanced students because the sky is the limit as far as technique goes. It is much more difficult and challenging to come up with level- and age-appropriate choreography. This is where it is helpful to have sources to which you can go for inspiration and find material that will make your students look good. It is a common mistake, especially with new teachers, to give students choreography and technique that they cannot possibly do correctly because of their lack of training. What typically happens in these instances is that the students look bad, and feel terribly uncomfortable and insecure—and consequently the number is not a success. Using the technique that they are learning in their classes is helpful to them, because they feel they can do it. That builds their confidence, which in turn enables them to become stronger and more accomplished. The bottom line is, if your students don't look good then neither do you! Many employers will make decisions about whether or not to keep their teachers for the following year contingent on how their numbers look in performance. The more successful your students are, the more trust they will develop with you as a teacher—and that will build as the years go by.

> "Real success is finding your lifework in the work that you love."
>
> *—David McCullough*

There is real truth in this quote because if you really do love what you are doing, you will not object to putting in the extra time necessary or extending yourself to help others when needed. Having a heart in your work will help you through the days when you are finding it difficult. Keeping in mind the joy and empowerment you can give to your students is extremely uplifting. Although the majority of our students will never dance professionally, we know that the life lessons and coping skills we instill in them will stand them in good stead for the rest of their lives—no matter their profession, or personal and professional relationships. How awesome is that? And yet what a tremendous responsibility lies in our hands.

Bravo! Act One Curtain Calls

Remember these things:

- Dance teachers need to think of themselves as a product or business
- If you are happy with where you are, then it's time to look closely at yourself and your worth professionally to see how much further you can go
- Think of what sets you apart from other teachers in your area
- The more knowledge you can acquire and the more experience you have, the more valuable you become to any employer
- Joining a teacher community can be extremely beneficial
- Trust yourself, trust your knowledge and trust your ability to teach
- Invest in printing professional cards with a description of what you do and with all of your contact information
- Always be well prepared so that you can create the right image for yourself through promotional materials, the way you dress and act
- Your employer needs to know that he or she can count on you to be where you should be when you are supposed to be there
- You need to establish your good name and then protect it
- If your students don't look good then neither do you!
- Having your heart in your work will help you through the days when you are finding it difficult to do so

How to Get Your Name in Lights—Act Two: **Steve Sirico**

> Today, and every day, deliver more than you are getting paid to do. The victory of success will be half won when you learn the secret of putting out more than is expected in all that you do. Make yourself so valuable in your work that eventually you will become indispensable. Exercise your privilege to go the extra mile, and enjoy all the rewards you receive. You deserve them!
>
> —*Og Mandino*

If you want to excel in all you do, follow the **"Three B's"** rule to improve your position and increase your value at any studio where you teach.

Be on time

Be professional

Be reliable

Sound's easy enough! Yet there are teachers who, for whatever reason, do not follow these simple rules for advancement.

During my years of teaching teachers at training programs, I have been asked many times by them, what it is that increases teachers' value to their employers and how can they create demand for themselves? I have always given them the "Three B's" rule. Of course, you need to have knowledge and be willing to learn, but without the Three B's, the rest really doesn't matter. As a teacher and studio owner, I have been on both sides. I know that as a teacher, you may sometimes feel unappreciated and taken for granted. Some of it may be true and some may be your perception. If this is an issue for you, go to the studio owner and tell him how you feel. I am amazed at how many times a teacher will not communicate his or her feelings.

As studio owners, we sometimes get busy or bogged down with the irritants of the week, and may seem a bit detached or disinterested. Try not to take it personally. It may be that little Susie's mom just gave us a problem about her account or her child's placement in class. It probably has nothing to do with you. However, left unattended, this one issue you are dealing with could create resentment and lead you, as a teacher, to start to become disenchanted with the owner. Ask to talk with the owner at a time when things are calm and do not be afraid to express your concerns. It is important to studio owners that their faculty feels good about working at their studio. As long as you are following those three golden rules you should stay employed for the mutually agreed time and much longer. There have been times when I have discovered a faculty member was unhappy for one reason or another over something that could have so easily been fixed—if there had been dialogue. Those whom you work for won't be perfect in every way, so it makes no sense for you to get angry with them and let it affect your work. Generally a calm conversation can overcome most obstacles. It can be hard to forget a perceived slight and go on to teach a killer class, but that is what makes you a professional. I have a pretty good idea from coaching studio owners exactly what they are looking for in a teacher. Knowledge is something every teacher needs to keep acquiring, as trends and styles change. Teachers must be in some kind of learning mode to continue to grow, and it is normally expected when you are hired that you will be willing to go with the times and continue to acquire knowledge.

No studio owner would hire you if he or she didn't think you were qualified and right for that studio. What will really make you an asset to the owner is if you can go that extra yard. If you act professionally and are reliable, you will be in demand and an asset to any business owner. It will also be easy when it is time to ask for a raise—as a matter of fact, you may get one without asking if you comply with these principles. Continue to grow and learn but above all don't lose sight of the most important fact: that even if you are the greatest teacher, with the most unique choreography or fun-loving personality, it is doubtful you will advance unless you are also complying with the "Three B's" rule. Studio owners just do not need the headaches!

It is human nature to want to be valued. To be valued at the workplace, you will need to show everyone why you should be valued. Sounds unfair? Well, that is just the way life works. First you pay, and then you receive. It happens in all areas of building your life's mission. First you go to school, then for some, on to college. Or you learn a trade, and then you work at that trade, putting in extra time if needed and doing it for minimal pay. Then you build to the point where you finally get noticed, you advance, and you finally have your payday! Think of any profession and that is the way it works. Chances are you have already spent a lot of time and years building up to where you are today.

So now how can you translate that into your moment?

Once you have put in the time and have shown a great attitude and are willing to go that extra mile, you will be noticed and your time to shine is at hand.

How do you increase your value to your employer and thus increase your earning power?

All of the tips in the last chapter will be the key for you to continue to help you increase your earning power. It is not just about showing up and teaching. It is about sharing and caring!

Tips To Make You Invaluable To Your Employer!

Your employer is eager to find the right people to be part of the team. Are you the right fit? Here is what I can tell you about the dance teaching profession. All dance studio owners are consumed with the mission to make each and every student have fun and learn. Using the tips below in your class will help you show your students how much you care!

Make eye contact. This also projects an image of confidence, concern and care. It tells students that you respect them, as well. Corrections will have a more lasting impact with eye contact. If you have given the same one over and over again, the right look can be the trigger that helps the student finally get it. Praise will also have more impact with the right eye contact.

Say my name, say my name! You may remember that song. The sweetest sound to any student's ears is the sound of his or her name being said, especially from an authority figure such as the teacher. We remind our faculty about this regularly. Find some way to say your students' names on a regular basis.

Have a great attitude. Everyone knows a positive attitude is important. After all, we can't expect our students to have one if we do not. The problem is that few people realize how important a role it plays in the way you communicate and the way you are perceived. Without a positive attitude, your words can be heard as cynical and fall on deaf ears. No one really cares about your issues, problems or mood swings. Leave them at the door before you walk into the building. A positive attitude and good disposition need to be present at all times. Hey, its showbiz, baby!

Take a genuine interest in your students. This is really where the rubber meets the road. If you are doing it purely for the paycheck, I can assure you, you will not last long or build a strong following. If you are teaching just to pacify your desire to choreograph or as a creative outlet, I recommend you get a job as a choreographer because your days are numbered as a teacher. To really enjoy teaching and to be a good teacher, you must take an interest in the students—and not just the good ones, but each and every one of them! Find out what makes each student tick, and you will gain a greater knowledge of who that person is. You will also learn more about who you are and how you can grow as a teacher. I still learn all the time from my students. That's one of the elements of teaching that I really enjoy. I have heard from many studio owners that they have trouble finding teachers who really care about the students. If you want to increase your earning power and build a great following, it really does depend on how much you care!

Building an Impeccable Reputation for a Lifetime

As a teacher the only thing you have that can make or break you is your reputation. How you conduct yourself with your boss and with your students, parents and fellow faculty says a lot about you.

Here is a key factor in your growth: If you are not conducting yourself in a professional manner, then you jeopardize your worth to your employer and your very employment.

Here are ways to make sure your reputation is impeccable:

1. **Always—and I mean always—be on time!** Even better, always be fifteen minutes early. Being late is the one factor that will drive your boss crazy. I don't care if you are the best teacher on the planet. If you can't be on time, I wouldn't hire you for anything, and I wouldn't recommend you to anyone either. In the dance school business, classes must start and end on time. Our clients are way too busy, running around shopping, picking up other kids and working. If a child's class is always starting late or finishing late, this will be an irritant. If you are always late, this will signal to your employer that you are not serious, that you can't be counted on and that you are unreliable—not the kind of reputation you need to have following you around. If you have been late in the past, make it your business to change or you will never achieve the kind of success you truly desire.

2. **Always be reliable.** This one pretty much goes in hand with the one above. If you fail at these two things, then nothing else will matter in your development as a dance teacher. Being reliable will show everyone that you are serious in what you do. It will make you a professional in the highest

degree. Think about any successful person, and I will show you one that knows you must be on time, reliable and a person of your word.

3. Do not befriend the students. This is so important nowadays. The last thing you want is for your students to know all about your personal life. This is a surefire way for you to have problems with the students, their parents and your boss. I hear about teachers e-mailing students, sending them text messages and having them be friends on one of the social networks. **BIG mistake!** If you have a Facebook page, I recommend that you set one up just for you as a teacher, where you can promote your classes, your work and your students. Use it as a tool to relay messages about who you are as a professional. Do not friend students on your personal account, where they can see you partying, making off-color comments, read about your daily woes or see what you do behind closed doors. I like Facebook, but it can be very dangerous to you as a professional if you are not careful. In any event, do you really want the students you teach to know what you are doing? This will not enhance your reputation as a professional. If you need to have children or teens as your friends, then you'd better find a new line of work!

4. Always be prepared. This may take you some time each week, but it will be a BIG key to successful classes. Think of it this way. If you were a surgeon, would you walk into surgery without any thought as to what procedure you were going to follow? Of course not! Make a plan each week, and proceed with the plan. Make it flexible so you can change direction if needed, but I recommend that you never go into a class not knowing what you are going to do. A well-thought-out class plan will make you a star at your school!

5. Continue to learn! It is one of the reasons Angela and I created Dance Teacher Web.com. For many years, we have taught for different teacher-training organizations and at teacher workshops and conventions. We have heard over and over how being a teacher can be very isolating and draining. It is easy to get a bit burned out if you are not careful. And it can come at the most inopportune time! Keep your creativity alive by finding out what your hot buttons are. Aside from watching dance, training videos and shows, find out where you are most at peace with yourself. Where do you feel the most freedom? Go there and bring a note pad and just think! You may even want to bring along your iPod music that stirs your creative juices. Go to seminars, conferences and any other place where like-minded professionals gather. Network, exchange ideas and learn. The best teachers are the ones who never stop learning!

6. **Don't be a complainer!** This is a real turnoff to any employer. If you have an issue then you need to believe in yourself and in the fact that you control change, and meet face-to-face with your employer to fix what is broken. You may be someone who does not like confrontation. Well guess what? No one wants confrontation. Who wakes up in the morning saying, "Oh boy, I really hope to have a real knock-down drag-out confrontation with someone today!" In life, things happen, but not everything that happens has to be a big drama unless we make it that way. If you have an issue and you can work to fix it, how empowering do you think that will be to you?

7. **Never try to take your employers' students!** This one really is a no brainer, but you see it time and time again. If you would like to open your own place, do it on your our own dime. Do not try to take the current students with you and especially not in the backyard of your current employer. Remember, you didn't spend any time or money to acquire those students. If you would like to open your own school, do it the right way. You may even want to consider approaching your current employer to talk to him or her about what you would like to do. Your employer may even be interested in being a part of your new venture. If you are a good teacher and have built a following, then you can do the same thing somewhere else. Keep in mind that if you do it the wrong way, then the same thing that you are doing to your employer could very possibly happen to you down the road. Think about how that would make you feel. I believe that what goes around comes around.

Make A Choice That From This Moment Forward...

You will be committed to being all you can be. That you will have the right mindset and you will always do what is right for your students and your employer. Your attitude is a big key to how you will be treated and how far you will advance. It will also determine how successful you are and how much earning power you will have. Now let that sink into your head for a while.

So the question is how is your attitude?

Do you need an attitude adjustment?

The good news is that you are in control of your thoughts, acts and deeds! Look, the reality is that if you are not happy where you are working, you need to get together with your employer and see if you can work it out. If not, it is probably best for all parties that you move on. No one is putting a gun to your head or saying that you must work for one person. If you are bitter, unhappy and unproductive, who is that really hurting? Mostly your reputation!

There is an old saying that "your reputation will precede you." Since it gets there first, let the news about you be a headline that reads, **"You are a wonderful, caring person who is reliable, professional and top-shelf in every way!"** Now how does that sound?

Bravo! Act Two Curtain Calls

Remember these things:

- Be on time, be professional and always be reliable
- Knowledge is something that every teacher needs to keep acquiring
- If an issue exists, be sure to have a talk with your studio owner before the issues gets bigger
- Your studio owner wouldn't hire you if he or she didn't think you were qualified and right for that studio
- Show why you should be valued at your workplace
- It is not just about showing up and teaching. It is about sharing and caring!
- Find ways to say the names of your students on a regular basis
- Be sure to leave your attitude at the door before you walk into the building
- Don't only take interest in the good students, but in all of your students
- Being a dance teacher means that you must always be prepared
- If you should stop working at your studio, don't take your students to a new one with you
- Make a commitment to be all you can be
- You are always in control or your acts, thoughts and deeds
- Your reputation will always precede you

How to Get Your Name in Lights—Act Three: **Robert Landau**

"Our destiny is not written for us, but by us."

—Barack Obama

The Parable of Suzanne

Suzanne had been a teacher for close to five years when all of a sudden, she decided one day to drop out of what seemed to have been a very promising career. She opted for something else—event planning! She figured it was a logical place to land after all those years because, aside from dance, orchestrating highly memorable events was a top interest. After a year of more downs than ups, Suzanne was finally making a name for herself in her city's event-planning world. Things were finally starting to look up. She knew that beginning a new business from scratch was going to take a while and it was certainly slow going at first. One thing started to lead to another, and she was off.

As her event momentum began to build, she noticed a certain pronounced feeling she would get every so often that she couldn't exactly identify. She only knew the feeling when it would make itself known to her. If she would just keep focused on what she was doing, the feeling would go away just as quickly as it had arrived. After a number of months of this feeling coming and going, she noticed that the feeling was lingering a little longer. In fact, there were some days when it would just stay with her, like a dark cloud hanging over her. This wasn't necessarily a bad thing, as it forced her to take a look at what was going on.

"OK, OK, already! I'll take a look on a deeper level and finally see what this darn dark cloud that seems to be following me is all about." Suzanne had actually taken to talking to the feeling, because it had been with her for so long that she felt it was a part of her. "So, if I had to put a label on what this feeling actually is, what would I call you?" She thought for a while, and then realized that the feeling was tinged with a heavy dose of emotion, negative emotion, this feeling of extreme sadness. "Wow, what IS this all about?" Suzanne wondered. At least she finally knew what type of feeling this was. Now she had to figure out what it was attached to, and she knew that one doesn't feel this amount of sadness for no reason.

After a couple of days had passed, an old friend of Suzanne's called her up and invited her to a grand opening event at a new dance studio. While grateful for the invitation, Suzanne's first inclination was to flat out turn it down. She didn't relish the thought of going back into the studio world, even if it was for one night. Her friend all but insisted. Suzanne promised that she would think about it.

Shortly thereafter, Suzanne began to notice something very strange occurring concerning her emotional state. Whenever she would feel the emotion of sadness overtake her, the only thing that would turn everything around was when she would think about going to the grand opening at the dance studio. "Now how could this be?" she thought. "I shouldn't really care one way or the other about the dance-studio world. I left that long ago. It's a done deal—it's over!"

That may have been the case but she started to realize that there was something that she missed about being a part of a dance-studio staff. She missed the teamwork and the expressions of challenge that her students had on their faces whenever one of her classes would begin. They knew, like she once did, that something special was going to happen. Suzanne had to admit to herself that there was something she missed about teaching the fine art of dance—and she came to a huge realization. Suzanne's frequent bouts of sadness had to do with missing being a dance teacher.

There were two things she decided to do to keep changing the sadness into happiness. First and foremost, she decided to go to the grand opening. Suzanne also decided that she would start a blog about teaching dance. "How ingenious!" she thought. "This way I can keep one foot in event planning and the other in the world of teaching dance. I'll even go one step further and make my blog something totally unique. I want it to stand out and be noticed. OK, OK—I have to finally admit to myself that event planning may not be everything I thought it was going to be. But even more important is the fact that I really do miss teaching like crazy! I will put all that energy into my blog and see what happens. If nothing else, it'll be a lot of fun, something I seem to be missing in my life at the moment."

Suzanne had no idea how easy it was to create her own WordPress blog site, and had loads of fun picking exactly how the blog would look and what the domain name would be. She spent hours finding artwork and photographs that she could use to augment the posts that she would soon create.

Her creative muse was really put to the test in a way that event planning hadn't for her. Not that there was anything wrong with event planning—she just knew once and for all where her heart really felt happy and free. Dance was her passion. Teaching was the way her passion had manifested, and even though that may have been many years ago, Suzanne felt as if she was honoring her passion once again by creating her blog.

"I gotta have an angle. To stand out, I should have some sort of a gimmick. But one that's honest and true. Let me think about this . . . let me think. What would work? What would keep my interest and that of readers?" Just then, as if someone heard her thoughts, she got the answer she had been waiting for. "Oh this is SO COOL! I'm going to write about different cultures and how dance is taught in those countries. I will look for what unifies each culture in the name of dance, all the while focusing on what's important in dance education in each of those places. I'll delve into the history of dance and how it has evolved in each culture. Then I'll tie it all into how, through dance teachers, the tradition of dance is kept alive in each country." Suzanne always had a love for doing research. Now she could put her love of research to work for her blog.

After only a month of intense preparation, her blog went "live." She monitored how many visits she got on her blog as the weeks passed. She decided that she would create two blog posts per week and see what happened. She also, with the help of a friend, figured out how to use keywords to get her blog noticed on the web. With whatever extra money she had, she advertised her blog in social media so people with common interests would know of her blog's existence. An intensive Twitter campaign was also created, with links to her various blog posts. In no time at all, all of her hard work was starting to pay off. She could see it by looking at the stats that showed her how many people were visiting her blog site and from the positive comments so many of them made in response to each posting. Suzanne was overjoyed to learn that so many readers wanted to subscribe to her blog so they wouldn't miss each new post that would hit the web waves!

There was one other way Suzanne knew that her blog was a hit. When she attended the grand opening of the new studio in her city with her friend, her friend introduced Suzanne as an ex-dance teacher and current blog poster. When people would ask her what her blog was all about, she was stunned to learn that many of the people she met that night had read a blog post of hers and had subscribed. It was at that party that someone who was an avid fan of her blog made a suggestion that to Suzanne, had struck gold.

"I LOVE your blog Suzanne!" the fan had said. "But may I give you a suggestion?" Suzanne was all ears. "Why don't you interview some of the prominent dance teachers in the countries that you write about? You could record it via the web and even better, you might have video footage of the interview be a part of the proceedings. This way you would add a whole other dimension to this wonderful mission of yours. Give it some thought Suzanne. It just might work."

Suzanne didn't have to think for a second. She couldn't wait to get home and figure out how she was going to incorporate this brilliant idea into her blog site offerings. As you might have guessed by now, it didn't take long for Suzanne to feature some really incredible teachers that were passionate about doing their thing in such far off places as Sri Lanka, Western Samoa and Bangkok—just to name a few. Suzanne also figured out a way to combine the various ideas about teaching dance that she had used in her classes way back when with the very same types of ideas that her interviewees were now using in their classes on the other side of the globe. Now even more people were taking notice of her blog and unbeknownst to her, Suzanne was beginning to develop quite a global reputation as a teacher of the fine art of dance. Along with this, something very interesting was beginning to happen, and it was something that Suzanne couldn't have been happier about.

Every so often, Suzanne would get an email or a phone call about a job offer. If you think those offers had to do with event planning, think again. The offers had everything to do with Suzanne teaching dance. A publishing company approached her to write a book about how and why dance is taught to keep cultures alive the world over. How did she feel about this?

"The joy in my heart was overwhelming. I would lie awake in my bed at night, unable to fall asleep. I was so excited about how things had turned out. To get the feedback I'd been getting was nothing short of astounding to me. I've learned such a huge lesson as I've walked this journey. It's a journey of believing in myself and realizing that low self-esteem is only as real as I choose to make it. There was no need to be my own worst enemy. Now I understand that each one of us has something special inside to offer the world. This can be done in a creative way that actually informs and creates awareness that in turn leads to change. This is something that the world needs right now, and I'm glad I can make my little contribution. I always had this inside of me, but I was the one that was keeping it hidden. I also never knew how much teaching dance had meant to me. All of those years of teaching a million classes, not getting much praise for it and having to deal with so many things that I had allowed to bring my spirits down. The odd thing I've realized is that my spirits couldn't have gotten too low because the flame for my true love, teaching dance, never died. I thought it did but the passion deep within kept the flame burning. Event planning was wonderful, but it wasn't my reason for being. Teaching dance IS, and you know what? I wouldn't have it any other way. I don't care about ever being a millionaire. Leave that to others. That's not my path, and I'm truly OK with that. I am enriched in my soul, that's where my wealth, my abundance lies. And it dances with my passion on a daily basis! If you would ever have told me where I'd wind up today doing what I've been doing with this blog and what's come of it, I would have laughed you right out of town! But look! It's almost obnoxious, because I now walk around with a permanent smile on my face. It's a smile that's connected with my passion, which is connected to my heart, which is connected to my love of teaching dance. It's an art, and it's something that is an important part of every culture and society on this planet of ours. I'm so honored to be a part of it."

How about you?

If you are looking for ways to be memorable and stand out, take a cue from Suzanne. She reconnected with her true passion, and all at once an incredible flow of creativity emerged. Suzanne reconnected with something she thought was long gone and out of that, found a really unique way to stand out and get recognized. She might not have originally wanted to, but what ended up happening in her case was that she created a real buzz in her city, and around the world. If she can do it, so can you! Suzanne created some really great ways of getting herself out there and the results were, and still are, incredible. Using her talents for sharing, writing, posting, creativity, marketing through social media and interviewing, she shed new light on what being a dance teacher around the world is all about.

So where is Suzanne now? Because of her newfound recognition, she's entertaining a number of offers to teach dance in her city and around the world. Suzanne would like to teach at a studio where she can once again hone her craft and then take things to the next level. "It's all about the journey, not the destination," she often says. She wants to combine so much of what she's learning from other teachers around the world into her style of teaching. Once that is said and done, Suzanne wants to open her own studio where her passion for her art can continue to motivate all those that cross her path. She also plans to keep her blog going indefinitely.

Suzanne was recently asked to share some words of advice for those in her beloved industry, and here's what she had to say: "Don't ever forget how important the job that you do is through each and every class you teach. Sure there are going to be many days when you want to throw in the towel. When you think you might be getting close to doing so, take a step back, breathe, and think again. Or, do what I did. Channel your energy into finding new ways to create a buzz about yourself so that others will perk up and take notice. It's truly a fun thing to do. I treat it like a class project that never ends. Through my art I am truly rejuvenated, and if that's the effect it has on my spirit, I know that it's having the same effect on everyone I touch each and every day. To me, that's what life is all about."

Amen to that!

Bravo! Act Three Curtain Calls

Remember these things:

- If you are looking for ways to be memorable and stand out, reconnect with your true passion—and all at once an incredible flow of creativity will emerge
- It's all about the journey, not the destination
- Don't ever forget how important the job that you do is through each and every class you teach
- On the days when you want to throw in the towel, take a step back, breathe, and think again
- Channel your energy into finding new ways to create a buzz about yourself so that others will perk up and take notice
- Through your art, you can always rejuvenate yourself
- Rejuvenating yourself has a direct effect on your spirit
- If your spirit and energy are constantly refreshed and renewed, you will feel it, as will everyone who crosses your path that day

NOTES

Chapter 7

The Role of a Lifetime

The Role of a Lifetime—Act One: **Angela D'Valda Sirico**

> "Our goals can only be achieved through a vehicle of a plan, in which we must fervently believe, and upon which we must rigorously act. There is no other route to success."
>
> —*Pablo Picasso*

The day you decided to become a dance teacher was the day you started an exciting journey, with many ports of call to new and exciting places. Whatever your reason for becoming a teacher, remember that you have chosen a profession where you have the privilege of influencing young people's minds, and helping them form their thoughts and bodies in a very positive way. Our students look to us for many things, from helping them with their talent and technique to showing them how to make quick decisions and build coping skills. They see us as role models for life in general. That is quite a responsibility, and yet it is exciting. What a wonderful experience it can be to help mold another human being, just as a sculptor would shape a piece of clay. Sometimes I believe that we really do not understand our impact on the young people around us. But if we even have a small inkling of how our interactions affect the students we teach, we have to be very thankful and appreciative of the role that we have been placed here to play.

I remember some years ago giving this impassioned speech to one of our most talented students. My goal was to try to get him to dance from the inside out and to really share his feelings with his audience. I wasn't a hundred percent sure that he was really paying attention to what I was saying, but when I had finished he looked at me and said, "Wow! You are really good at that!" At the time, it made me smile because working with this dancer was so rewarding. He had talent and was such a creative individual. I didn't see myself as a motivational speaker, but somehow I did get through to him, and I saw that he had listened and understood. That alone gave me a lot of confidence in the knowledge that I had acquired throughout my life as a dancer and teacher. This particular young man went on to be one of the stars of the classical world of dance. I remember thinking to myself that this teaching business really did have some extremely rewarding moments!! It's a great feeling to groom someone from a young age, and then release him or her to fly alone, confident and independent, and moving forward in their own best direction!

Let's find out a little about you!

- What do you really want out of your life?
- Are you looking for a better paying job?
- Are you interested in prestige?
- Do you like working with all ages and types of students, or is there one particular sector that you would prefer to work with?
- Do you want to teach in a studio or school setting?
- Do you want to teach on the conference or convention circuit?
- Where do you see yourself by next year?
- Where do you see yourself within the next five years?
- What do you feel that you need to work on or improve upon?
- Do you want a better personal life?

There may be other questions to ask yourself—think of it as a fact finding mission. The more you know about yourself and how you want to improve your life, the easier it will be to take action!

> "Crystallize your goals. Make a plan for achieving them and set yourself a deadline. Then, with supreme confidence, determination and disregard for obstacles and other people's criticisms carry out your plan."
>
> —*Paul J. Meyer*

Take some time to figure out what exactly your goals are, and then make a plan that includes a definite deadline. Without the deadline, the plan will go nowhere. It is important to hold yourself accountable so that there is a reason to keep moving forward. Of course it is helpful if you have a spouse or significant other, a good friend or partner to help keep you on track. I know, life gets busy, and it is always a challenge to find time to work on your plan. Try not to let yourself become sidetracked, and throw out that bag of excuses holding you back. There really is no time like the present. I do believe that it is helpful to write your thoughts down, whether they are about a new idea or your goals or your lesson plan. When you can see it in front of you, it somehow makes it more real and should spur you on to action. It is easy to drift along day-to-day, putting off what you should be doing for another day. But even if you accomplish some part of your plan each day, you will soon move forward and up to the next level. Be demanding of yourself, and keep your goals clearly in your mind at all times. Don't let that vision of a better life fade away—keep it fresh and active.

Once you have established the direction, start to make concrete plans to help you move. Perhaps you are very content with where you are now, and there is absolutely nothing wrong with that. But there is still always room for improvement, whether artistically, in business or in our personal lives. Dance teachers sometimes forget that they are a business—after all we do what we do for the love of it. But there is no reason why you should not make an excellent wage and be fulfilled in many directions. It is easy to get stuck in a rut, and that is not good for you, your students or your employer. There are always new things to learn, new places to go and stronger relationships to form. Why not make yourself more valuable to your employer so that there is a possibility of increasing your salary? Why not make yourself more valuable to your students so that your classes are full of eager, willing-to-learn dancers? Why not make yourself the best that you can possibly be? Don't let the fear of the unknown, or complacency, hold you back from a rewarding and enjoyable life.

> "Just as your car runs smoothly and requires less energy to go faster and further when the wheels are in perfect alignment, you perform better when your thoughts, feelings, emotions, goals and values are in balance."
>
> —*Brian Tracy*

Balance is the key to good dancing and a good life.

Without balance, it is difficult to maintain happiness both at work and at home. Of course, finding balance is not, as we know, always easy. But only by having a definite plan for every aspect of your life will you achieve the right balance for you. Remember, what works for one might not work for another, and it is only by doing some soul searching that you will realize what works for you and the people closest to you. There are no "wrongs" and "rights." It is totally up to you to discover how you need to structure your life. Surrounding yourself with people who are on your same wavelength will certainly be helpful, and planning moments when you can just get away from it all and relax are as important as going to work.

> "No one lives long enough to learn everything they need to learn from scratch. To be successful, we absolutely, positively have to find people who have already paid the price to learn the things that we need to learn to achieve our goals."
>
> —*Brian Tracy*

Seeking ways to further educate ourselves is a must. Discovering people who have travelled the road before us can be a big help.There is no end to learning, and as we learn, we open up doors to a world that perhaps we had no idea existed. Why limit yourself? You never know exactly in which direction life will take you. So why not be as prepared as possible for any eventuality? Isn't the joy really in continuing to learn? To teach successfully, it is imperative to keep learning. There are many different avenues to take to pursue further education, and in this era, it is easy to find the avenue for you by simply investigating on the Internet. Whatever you decide upon, take the action needed to make it happen. Don't wait for the "right" moment—it may never come! Find a way to make it work, and you will be extremely thankful that you did.

So now we have set our goals and put a plan into action. What is next? Really, just more of the same! If you find you are not reaching your goals, then it is probably time to adjust your attitude and way that you are thinking so that you can make an alternate plan. There are no easy answers to anything in life, and it is all about being flexible and willing to change. Keep in mind how great the rewards can be in every aspect of your life if you persevere. Count your blessings and be happy for any progress that you are making. Although we constantly need to be thinking ahead, it is just as important to enjoy your life each day.

> "What you get by achieving your goals is not as important as what you become by achieving your goals."
>
> *—Henry David Thoreau*

How true this is!

The more we work on ourselves, the more we can give to others and the better sense of fulfillment we will experience. The world is ready for the new and improved you, so go for it and most importantly, enjoy the journey!

Bravo! Act One Curtain Calls

Remember these things:

- It's a wonderful experience to help mold another human being—just as a sculptor would mold a piece of clay
- We have to be very thankful and appreciative of the role that we have been placed here to play
- Take some time to figure out what your goals are, and then make a plan that includes a definite deadline. Without the deadline, the plan will go nowhere
- Hold yourself accountable so that there is a reason to keep moving forward
- Don't let the fear of the unknown, or complacency, hold you back from a rewarding and enjoyable life.
- Balance is the key to good dancing and a good life
- There are no easy answers to anything in life. It is all about being flexible and willing to change
- The world is ready for the new and improved you, so go for it and most importantly, enjoy the journey!

The Role of a Lifetime—Act Two: **Steve Sirico**

"Why stop dreaming when you wake up?"

—*Walt Disney*

What a terrific question by the man who routinely turned his dreams into reality. I am sure he had many moments of doubt. But he never let that stop him for a minute. He knew if he had a dream and then worked out a plan and then had the courage to take action, he could do it! I recently watched a television show on the life of Walt Disney, and I was just so inspired with his work. I remember growing up and watching the *Wonderful World of Disney* on Sunday nights. I can remember the excitement when my parents took my sister, my brother and me to Disneyland in California and then to Disney World in Florida. All the movies, television shows and theme parks were the dreams of this one man—a man who developed a plan and then put it into **ACTION!**

Nothing else beats action. The person with the plan or goal that is a masterpiece is trumped every time by the person who has a lesser plan but takes action to move the plan forward. Walt Disney said as much in the interviews during this television show. You can't always have everything set up just right. If you wait for all of the lights to turn green, you will never leave your driveway. Don't let your dreams and goals stay as such. To turn anything you want to do into reality you must take **ACTION!**

So here are important questions I would like to ask you:

- What are your deepest dreams?
- Where do you want to go in your life?
- Where do you see yourself five years from now? How about ten?
- Do you have a plan to get you there?
- Do you think you can really achieve your dreams and goals?
- Do you take action?
- Will anything stop you from achieving your goals?

Teaching dance really is a wonderful profession. Think about how lucky we are. We get to create something new almost every day! We get to work with children of all ages and see them turn into young adults. We have an incredible influence over them. The skills we give them will enhance their lives no matter where their lives take them. Teachers spend a lot of time giving and need to take time to make sure that they are on track. Don't lose yourself in what you are doing, day in and day out. Make sure your life is headed in the direction that you want it to go!

Think about this!

To turn your dreams into goals and then into reality, you need a nonstop action plan!

Here are two ideas for developing your action plan. We have used this formula and found that it works for us both professionally and on a personal level. Since our professions are an extension of us, we need to align both of these—or your Yin and Yang will be out of whack!

A. Create a two-part mission statement. If you do not have one for your work, develop one as soon as possible. This mission statement will describe what you want your work life to be, your vision, and how those will impact your employer or business associates. Once you have done that, create a personal mission statement for what you want your job to do for you. It is very important because you will make all your decisions based on the principle of this personal mission statement. This may seem a bit selfish, but if your work does not serve you, then you will be swimming upstream your whole life.

B. Create goals and action plans. Once you have your mission statements set up, you can then start to focus on your goals and the plans you will make to achieve those goals. Make both professional and personal ones. I have found that the best way to do so is to make a list of goals on the right side of a piece of paper. Leave room in between each one. On the left-hand side of the paper, write down the action you intend to take to help you reach your goals. Now set a time frame in which these goals will be achieved. A tighter time frame is best, as it will make you work at your action plan with a bit more urgency.

Dance teachers are great at creating lesson plans for class and choreographing routines. So developing a plan like this will be a natural extension of what you do best. Just make sure that you put action behind your plan! Create your action plan, and write down your goals. Decide what action you can take that would help you meet your goals today, then in the next thirty days, six months or one year. Don't let your goals fall by the wayside.

Here are some pointers to consider in setting goals and achieving them.

Attitude plays a very big role in setting and achieving your goals. You must ask yourself if any part of you or your mind is holding you back from completing your simplest goals. Is there are any part of your behavior that is hindering you or putting your plans into disarray? If you do have problems in these areas, then the immediate thing to do is to address this problem.

Careers are made by good time management practice. Failing in a career is often attributed to bad time management. As a teacher, you need to think of the present and how far you want your teaching career to go.

Education is a BIG key in achieving your goals. Keep yourself in learning mode to avoid burnout and stagnation. We developed Dance Teacher Web.com to help give dance teachers continuing education and inspiration. Attend workshops, seminars and conferences that will help you recharge and get your creative juices flowing. This is not an expense but an investment in your continued growth and part of your action plan!

Personal financial situations also play a major role in achieving your goals. Have a realistic goal on how much you really want to earn. You also must create plans or stages by which you will reach your earning potential.

As the saying goes—'All work and no play makes Jill a dull girl', or something to that effect! Make sure that part of your goal planning includes time for yourself, when you will re-energize and reorganize your thoughts.

To start achieving your lifetime goals, set a quarter of a century plan, then break it down to five-year plans then break it down again to one-year plans, then six-month plans, then monthly plans, then weekly, then daily.

Then create a things-to-do list for the day. Always review your plans and prepare for contingencies. The basics of goal settings should not be so difficult once you get to be familiar with them.

How can you identify where you are and where you want to go?

It really is all about you. Many times people just wander through life and then, ten years later, wonder what happened. To develop a life plan that works for you, you will need to do a little digging to make sure you are happy with the path you are taking. Consider these pointers:

1. Know your purpose

Are you wandering through life with little direction—hoping that you'll find happiness, health and prosperity? Identify your life purpose or mission statement, and you will have your own unique compass that will lead you to your true north every time.

This may seem tricky at first when you see yourself to be in a tight spot or even a dead end. But there's always that little loophole that can turn things around, and make a big difference to your life.

2. Know your values

What do you value most? Make a list of your top five values. Some examples are security, freedom, family, spiritual development, learning. As you set your goals for the upcoming year, check your goals against your values. If the goal doesn't align with any of your top five values, you may want to reconsider it or revise it.

The number shouldn't discourage you. Instead it should motivate you to do more than you ever dreamed of doing. Dream big and have bold goals!

3. Know your needs

Unmet needs can keep you from living authentically. Take care of yourself. Do you have a need to be acknowledged, to be right, to be in control, to be loved? There are so many people who live their lives without realizing their dreams and most of them end up being stressed or even depressed for that matter. List your top four needs, and get them met before it's too late!

4. Know your passions

You know who you are and what you truly enjoy in life. Obstacles like doubt and lack of enthusiasm will only hinder you, but will not derail your chance to become the person you ought to be. Express yourself and honor the people who have inspired you to become the very person you wanted to be. I know that dance teachers have a big passion to teach. Don't let anything steal your joy!

5. Live from the inside out

Increase your awareness of your inner wisdom by regularly reflecting in silence. Commune with nature every chance you get to. Breathe deeply to quiet your distracted mind. For most city slickers, it's hard to find the peace and quiet we want, even in our own home. In my case, I often just sit in a dimly lit room and play some classical music. There's sound, yes, but music does soothe the savage beast.

6. Honor your strengths

What are your positive traits? What special talents do you have? List three. If you get stuck, ask those closest to you to help identify these. Are you imaginative, witty, creative or good with your hands? Find ways to express your authentic self through your strengths. You can increase your self-confidence when you can share what you know with others.

7. Serve others

When you live authentically, you may find that you develop an interconnected sense of being. When you are true to who you are, living your purpose and giving of your talents to the world around you, you give back in service what you came to share with others—your spirit—your essence. The reward for sharing your gift with those close to you is huge, and those people will appreciate what you have done for them.

Some of these topics may have caused you a bit of discomfort because they mean that you may need to create change in your life. Most of us equate change with pain! Hey, it is better to discover the true you and to live a happier, more fulfilling life, than to find out years later that your choices were not in your best interest. The difference lies within ourselves and how much we want to change for the better.

To move forward, take time to reflect!

It really is amazing how time passes by and how easy it is to lose touch with people who were important to us. These are the ones who have been instrumental in our successes as a teacher/choreographer/person. Take a moment this week or month to reconnect with those who have helped you. I recommend that you do so for several reasons.

As teachers we are always giving and sometimes do not realize what a difference we do make. How wonderful it is when a current or past student takes the time to say thank you for helping him or her. We have had students send us letters or come back years later who are now successful in business, as school teachers, dancers and moms. They say that their time training with us gave them invaluable lessons to help them to achieve great things in life. As dancers, it is especially rewarding to see past students who have gone on to be professional dancers or dance teachers. When they drop us a line, each word they write is as beautiful as the best poetry ever written. To hear from them how our words of encouragement and the invaluable life lessons we could give them, as teachers, were instrumental to their success, really touches our hearts.

If we reflect back, there is surely someone who has made a difference to us as a teacher. Now is a great time to let that teacher know. Call that person or write him or her a note say now how those words of wisdom had a positive impact on you. Remind your teacher of any anecdotes or technical knowledge that was particularly helpful to your development. This is great for former teachers to receive, and it will be good for you also. Whenever I write one of these letters, I find myself laughing and remembering all of the good times and lessons learned. I know I would not be where I am today if it were not for teachers who were passionate about teaching and about helping me. No one becomes a success on his or her own, and it doesn't happen overnight. Some teachers may question if they are successful or not. The truth is that if you teach and have students who listen and care about you, then you are successful—and don't doubt that for a moment.

Any time is a good time to thank co-workers who have helped you, and your boss for giving you an opportunity to work. Let that person know you care and appreciate him or her. When you reconnect with those who have helped you in the past, you may be surprised to find that they can also help you now. We have been given the opportunity to help and provide ongoing support to some of our students who have reconnected with us. I am still in touch with the teachers who helped me early on, and who continue to give me their knowledge and connections to this day.

Another reason to reconnect is that we never know when our time here on earth will be over. No one is promised a tomorrow. It would be tragic if you had been meaning to write a letter to a former teacher, but never got around to it and then discovered that that person had passed on. Recently we received news of the death of one of our former students. He was a young man with so much to live for. He had a lot of talent, but life had beaten him down, and he found he could not continue. It made me think of how we are all connected in life as teachers, students and friends. This young man visited our studio not so long ago, and whenever we talked, we would always reminisce about the great times we had together. He would tell us that our words and classes had influenced him positively in his life, both professionally and personally. After receiving the terrible news about him, we wished we had reached out to him more and perhaps give him additional words of wisdom to help him through a difficult time in his life. We do know, however, that his happiest times were when he was at our studio, training and being part of a great group of dancers. If anyone has made a difference to you, as a dancer or teacher—and there may be several— share that with him or her. You could call the person, but I think a hand-written letter has more impact, especially in today's world of e-mail and instant messaging.

The day will come, once you have been teaching for awhile, when out of the blue, you may receive a letter or note in the mail from a former student. Once you get through reading it, you too will know what a difference you have made in that person's life. After you wipe away the tears, you will also understand what an impact it makes on someone when you take the time to let that person know how instrumental to your success he or she was. Pass it on!

Bravo! Act Two Curtain Calls

Remember these things:

- The person with the plan or goal that is a masterpiece is trumped every time by the person who has a lesser plan but takes action to move the plan forward
- If you wait for all of the lights to turn green, you will never leave your driveway
- To turn anything you want to do into reality you must take **ACTION!**
- Make sure your life is headed in the direction that you want it to go!
- Decide what action you can take that would help you meet your goals today, then in the next thirty days, six months or one year
- Attitude plays a very big role in setting and achieving your goals
- Failing in a career is often attributed to bad time management
- To develop a life plan that works for you, you will need to do a little digging to make sure you are happy with the path you are taking
- If you teach and have students that listen and care about you, then you are successful

The Role of a Lifetime!—Act Three: **Robert Landau**

> "Without goals, and plans to reach them, you are like a ship that has set sail with no destination."
>
> —*Fitzhugh Dodson*

Not too long ago, I had a conversation with a dance teacher on the topic of setting goals. She had mentioned that to set a goal and to be sure that it actually happens, listing things one wants to change might achieve success. I agreed, but with a few stipulations. Thinking you want something to change and actually taking the steps necessary to see that change through can be two totally different things. It all comes down to the reason why so many of us don't see our wishes, hopes and dreams come true. It has everything to do with the difference between saying you'll do something and actually doing what it is you originally said you would do.

So here's something to consider. I was recently speaking to a large group of people about the topic of setting goals. I asked them to think of ten things they said they'd do over the last month or so. How many of those ten things actually ended up manifesting in their physical world? A few responded by saying five out of ten, more said two to four, but most said only one or two at the most. "So why do you think this is?" I asked. The most common answer I got in return had to do with the fact once the wish was made, nothing else was done to see it through. There was no follow-up. In other words they stated what they wanted to occur in the near future, but then dropped the ball because they didn't take the steps necessary to see it through to completion.

I thought about this for a while because so many times in my own life experience, I was faced with the very same results when I wanted a whole bunch of goals to manifest themselves into my life's path. What I realized was that the most common issue we have when we set goals up is the fact that we don't take the necessary steps to see them through. We say something and certainly mean it at the time, but then we all too often just leave things there, expecting someone or something else to swoop in and, like magic, turn our statements of dreams suddenly into reality—just like that! We often feel disappointed when things don't magically happen, and we wonder why we are continually left in the dark when it comes to our wishes, hopes and dreams. What good is making a resolution if it isn't seen through to completion? We are wasting our time and setting ourselves up for disappointment if we only get the job half done. It's like asking a question without ever getting the answer.

Any goal that you want to set in motion has two parts to it—the "saying" of it and the "doing," or the seeing through of it. My mother always used to say, "Don't say you'll do something unless you are actually prepared to see it through!" What she was saying was that I always need to say what I mean but also mean what I say. How right she was. But how do you make a goal for yourself and make sure it comes to pass? The same way you teach a student a dance routine. There are usually two parts to this type of a teaching process. First you state what it is that you want your student to learn. But as you very well know, saying it is only half the battle. Most of the time you need to show your students what you are talking about, so they can see how to do the routine. Once the student sees you do it, then he or she will get up and do it, too. In so doing, you make sure that he or she understands exactly what you were demonstrating, and you can fix anything that doesn't look right. So now the goal has been realized. You stated your intention and then saw it through to completion. You put actions to the original words you stated, and the job was complete. One step can't exist without the other. When you make a goal, you must take the steps necessary to see it through. It's got to be actualized—otherwise your original request just melts away in thin air. Making sure your words have the proper support after you've stated them is exactly how you go about realizing a goal.

How many times have you said something and then not taken the steps to make sure it happens? If you are like me, probably more times than you'd care to admit. We are only human, so saying things without a follow-up to see if what we said is being realized is often part of what we do. We have the power to change that, and it's up to us to do it. How so? It's actually easier than you might think.

When you state a goal that you'd like to see happen, state it and then outline the various steps you'll take to make sure that it comes to pass. Here's an example; say you want to help attract more students to study at the dance studio where you teach. The studio's been doing fine, but you really want to look at more ways to shine as a teacher there. So you figure that finding a way to get more students into your studio to study with you will do the trick. Now you say your goal out loud after formulating it in your mind, and you even write it down: "I will (not "want to") get twenty-five new students into these doors within the next six months. Most of these new students will end up studying with me, since I'll be teaching jazz by that time." Great! You are now halfway there. As I've already stated, what's the use of saying something like this if you aren't going to take the steps to make it happen? That's Part Two of the formula. So here's how that might look and what you might say to yourself to make things happen:

1) In a week's time I'll have a plan as to how I'm going to let the world know that I'll be teaching jazz at my studio and why perspective students should study with me

2) Once my plan is ready, I need to make sure it has dates as to when I'll have my main mode of publicity, social media ads ready, and the dates when they'll appear—and the tracking I'll do to see if those ads have brought in any takers

3) By the fifth month of my campaign, I'll re-evaluate to see where I'm at and how things are going. If I need to step things up a notch or two, or change some parts of my strategy, I'll figure out what to do based on where things are at that point in time

4) Most important of all, I will NOT drop the ball. I fully expect to see at least twenty-five new students in my new jazz class when all is said and done. I will hold myself to the days and dates I've set up in my timeline and make sure things are always moving forward

What's the most important aspect of this plan? Seeing it through! This is close to the goal-setting plan that the dance teacher I first mentioned in this chapter created to get more students to study with her. It worked only because she stuck to her word and made sure that things were happening. She kept her word to herself and fully understood that the only way she was going to be successful was using the two-part goal-setting process. And that entails stating what you want to occur and then making sure that it does—according to the steps you plan to take to get there. Just as in the example above, she assigned specific future dates and times regarding when certain steps toward the success she was looking for would be accomplished. When the small steps were successful, she got all the encouragement she needed to know that her end-result was near.

So here's the question—how are you when it comes to setting goals for your teaching practice, as well as for the rest of your life? If realizing your goals isn't all it could be, why not follow some of the key points I've emphasized here? You'll be more than happy with the results. All it takes is logically planning out how you'll get from point A to point B. The key is not just talking about getting there but actually figuring out in a logical way exactly how you'll arrive at the finish line, step by step, and on what day, date and time of day you'll accomplish each step. If a certain step doesn't turn out the way you planned, no problem. Just find an alternative way of getting there. There's more than one way to get to where you need to be. Flexibility is the key that unlocks the door to ultimate success.

Here are a couple of other points you might want to keep in mind when it comes to making a resolution or goal. See and feel the end result as if it's here with you right now. Here's what I mean. Say you set a goal to lose weight. According to the process we've been looking at in this chapter, you'd ask yourself how much you want to lose and what schedule you will adopt to gauge when the pounds will start to drop off. What methods of weight loss will you use to get there? What steps will you take to see it through? By what days and dates will you lose what you need to lose? Most important, how will you feel and look once you've achieved your goal? Seeing the 'future' as if it's already here is a huge tool that you should always use to bring things to you. If you want the perfect job or the perfect mate, if you want to teach the perfect class season after season after season, what steps will you take on what days and months along the journey to make your dream a reality? How will it feel right here, right now, once you've gotten there? The trick is to see your dream, your goal, your resolution realized each day before you go to sleep and each morning just before you get out of bed. That can be the hardest part because you are asking your mind to consider something that is not yet in the present. Just do it anyway! Put it out there and feel good whenever you do and you just might be overjoyed to see what you'll eventually get in return.

Be patient! That's one of the hardest pieces of this puzzle. We want things to appear shortly after we've asked for them rather than being O.K. with the time it actually takes to make the wish a reality. Keep the end always in sight, and you'll get there. Sometimes the exact steps will be filled in for you. The more you stay out of the way the better. Know that you'll get there, that's the important thing.

Within each moment lies a world of possibilities. That's truly an amazing fact, isn't it? What also lies within each moment is unlimited potential. How do you realize it? By making sure your intention is clear and focused. The second part of realizing has to do with believing your goal will indeed occur—feeling what it is you want even before it has happened. That expectation, that knowing, sends out strong signals to manifest your desire. Upon hearing what it is that you want in your life, the Universe immediately goes to work making your dream come true.

Don't believe you can do something? Well, maybe that's the problem. The fact that you don't think or feel that you can do something literally means nothing will happen unless you change your mindset. Thoughts of future actions can indeed be scary, but you have to move past whatever fears might come up so you can get to accomplish the task at hand. If you don't believe you can do something, that's the message you are sending to The Universe, and it knows nothing more than to respond to your 'wish' in kind. You get what you ask for.

How do you move past a belief that is negative and self-defeating in nature? You just do it! If you don't think you can do a task that is right before you, just change the thought process connected to your disbelief. If you felt differently about the situation, could you indeed do what you originally thought was beyond your reach? Instead of saying, "I don't think I can do that," change that up to this: "I definitely DO think I can do that!" Even if you don't know how that will physically happen, create the mental expectation by saying that affirmation over and over. Don't be surprised if you start feeling that you can do what was once thought to be impossible. Make sure you know that you deserve it and that you allow it to happen. If you start to feel that you can do it, energies shift and rework themselves in your favor, and lo and behold, you'll find that what you once refused to believe was possible is unfolding without any resistance right before your eyes. Is it magic? Yes! It's the magic of belief and the knowing that things are possible if you think and feel they are. You can do it—just get out of your way and let it happen. Put one foot in front of the other and move forward. That's what achieving goals is all about.

Once you've made this work for yourself, how powerful would it be to pass some of this knowledge on to your students? What we're talking about here are powerful tools that can be used to change lives. If you believe it works for you and can become walking proof that it does, then others will want to know what that pep in your step is all about. If they knew how to create change in their lives by realizing the goals they have hoped and longed for, how powerful would that be for you to share this with them?

All of this and more can occur once you put some simple goal-realizing tools into place. Make it work for yourself first. You'll feel so much better once you have. From there you can pass this knowledge on to those whom you teach and love. Part of being here has everything to do with realizing how powerful you really are. You can indeed change things for the better, in and out of the studio classroom. But it won't happen on its own. You have to take the ship's wheel and steer your vessel to where you want to be. With clear intent and the planning of exactly how to get there, you can be a true teacher, a leader and role model for others and for yourself. When you really think about it, isn't that what life is all about anyway?

Bravo! Act Three Curtain Calls

Remember these things:

- Thinking you want something to change and actually taking the steps necessary to see that change through can be two totally different things
- Don't say you'll do something unless you are actually prepared to see it through
- When you state a goal that you'd like to see happen, state it and then outline the various steps you'll take to make sure it comes to pass
- There's more than one way to get to where you need to be. Flexibility is the key that unlocks the door to ultimate success
- See and feel the result of what you are wishing for as if it's here with you right now
- See your dream, your goal, your resolution realized each day before you go to sleep and each morning just before you get out of bed
- Patience is the key to manifestation
- Within every moment lies unlimited possibilities and potential
- If you don't believe you can do something, that's the message you are sending out
- You get what you ask for
- You can do it—just get out of your way and let it happen. Put one foot in front of the other and move forward. That's what achieving goals is all about
- You have to take the ship's wheel and steer your vessel to where you want to be

NOTES

Chapter 8

Encore! Encore!

Encore! Encore! Act One: **Steve Sirico**

> Don't limit yourself. Many people limit themselves to what they think they can do. You can go as far as your mind lets you. What you believe, you can achieve.
>
> —*Mary Kay Ash*

M.I.W.—the wonderful acronym we use for our dancers that stands for: **M**ake **I**t **W**ork!

When you think about, it isn't that what teaching is about? We teach our students to cultivate this mentality and as teachers show this in all we do. That is show biz and, as a matter of fact, that's what life is about! A can-do attitude will take you places you can't even imagine.

Remember: Your attitude determines your actions or inactions. Your outlook will determine your life's outcome more than any other single factor!

WARNING: Beware of those who will try to knock you down!

There are two kinds of people in the world.

There are doers and the naysayers.

The doers are the ones who will lend support, tips, solutions, ideas and encouragement when you need it most!

The doers are people you will meet along the way who will be eager to lend support and sensible advice. They will also be people from your past who have invested time and love into helping you achieve.

The naysayers focus on what is wrong with you, your ideas or plan, rather than what is right with it.

Naysayers possess a doubting spirit.

Naysayers hate change.

Naysayers talk behind your back and hate to see others succeed.

Naysayers cause dissension.

Naysayers will try to make your life a misery.

The key here is to look closely at the associations in your life, for that is the direction in which you are heading. In other words, choose your associates with great care and avoid the naysayers at all costs!

Fill your life and your career with doers. Build your circle with doers, and you will move forward. If you have people around you who are always trying to pull you down, you will not reach your full potential. Get these people out of your life and career, and watch how you FLY!

YOUR Attitude determines YOUR actions.

You are not what you think you are. What you think, you are!

Tell me your vision of your life and career, and I will tell you your future. If you want to change your career or your life, change your vision. Build a picture in your mind of what your ideal career or life would look like, be like, and you will bring it to life. Seems too simple or unbelievable? Think again! Keep this new picture in your mind 24/7, and expect that blimps will come along the way. This should not and must not deter you. Life isn't always easy or fair, so what?—you are the master of your life!

Staying Connected

Recently Angie and I had the opportunity to visit our long-time family friend and mentor, Fred Favorite. Fred had an amazing career as a professional dancer, choreographer, show producer and teacher. His many credits include performing in the Bob DeVoye Trio that starred as guest artists with Liberace, on *The Ed Sullivan Show,* and toured the world and appeared in all of the top theaters and nightclubs as a headline act. He and Bob helped Angie and I develop our act and gave us our first job in one of their terrific productions as a featured act and lead dancers. I have personally known Fred since I was a very young boy.

We love Fred, and he is family to us. It does not matter how much time has passed since we last saw him—we'll always pick up right where we left off. Aside from all the great memories and laughs we have, he always lends wonderful support and encouragement. His insight and passion for dance and life is as valuable today as it was many years ago. Now in his eighties, he is such a joy to be with and talk to. I love to tap into his knowledge and to hear the wonderful stories. I recommend that you connect and reconnect with your friends and mentors. They are the ones who will rejoice most in your achievements—after all, they have played a BIG part in where you are today and where you will go tomorrow.

Remember you did not get to where you are today on your own. Someone has helped you to get to where you are and they may very well continue to do so. Sometimes when we look back, it helps us to move forward. Lessons learned on the journey, with all the ups and downs, should help you to develop your life plan. If you get nothing else out of this book, I hope you will decide today to create a life plan that becomes the road map to take you where you want to go. Be bold, and share that plan with your close circle of doers who want to see you succeed and are thrilled by your advancement. And once you have developed that plan, the time to proceed is NOW! Don't wait—the best time to make your move is today. Procrastination is the biggest enemy you will face on your life's journey.

Be All You Can Be!

This was a slogan made famous by the U.S. Army during one of its recruiting campaigns. It should be your personal mission statement. The only way to advance is to stretch, and I am not talking about improving your split! Rubber bands come in all sizes, but to be effective, they must be stretched. Like rubber bands, we have different personalities but must stretch to be effective. John Maxwell has written that 95 percent of people avoid stretching. The main reason? Most of us are vulnerable when we are stretching. When you put yourself out there, you encounter problems and issues. You draw criticism along the way, but you will know you are making progress when you receive the most resistance. Another reason we avoid stretching is because it will involve change. Change can be uncomfortable and may mean you will need to grow. But that is what great teachers teach! To evolve and to advance in all you do, you must continue to stretch!

Most people never learn that stretching never stops. I understand the need for recuperation and restoration, but problems develop when we stretch a little and rest a lot. Too often dancers believe that once they become teachers, their education is over. To be great, understand that the days of learning and discovery never end. A good dance education or any education for that matter does nothing more than to teach us to stretch and learn for the rest of our lives. Don't ever fall into the mindset of, "Oh I know that," or "What can they teach me that I don't already know," or "I tried that once." The happiest people in the world are growing people. Angela and I wanted to be able to help dance teachers grow, learn and advance and to give them a place to go where they could receive inspiration and practical help at the click of a button. Never stop learning, growing and advancing, and you will never burnout!

The Need For Positive Affirmation

Find time to talk to yourself, and make sure you speak in terms of positive affirmations. You will have doubts along the way, and if you are not careful, you will think and even worse speak negatively about yourself and your career. Yes, you may even encounter failure along the way. But don't ever let failure become final. Be aware that discouragement is failure's partner. The doers in your life will help you pull out of those discouraging moments. Keep in mind that during those down times, one of the best ways to help yourself is through helping others. Become an encourager! The best time to support others is when they are stretching themselves. Many times people wait too long to lend support and as a result are too late. I think there are times we are reluctant to encourage risk takers, because in doing so we identify with them. In other words we go out on a limb with them. If they fail, we fail too! I believe that you should encourage early and often. If you see a friend or colleague slipping, jump right in and lend him or her some practical help. Don't hesitate to give support in front of others as nothing is more helpful than giving honest praise in front of your peers. Write down some positive affirmations that speak to you and read them daily. Hey, some days will be harder than others. I'll bet if you look back on even your darkest days you will have found out a lot about yourself—and will find valuable lessons that will enhance your life as you move forward. Sometime we make mistakes. Don't be too hard on yourself. Put it into your "lessons learned" library and move on.

Your Journey Is Your Life!

Most people will look back on their lives and remember fondly some of the tough times they endured. They consider lessons learned and how those times are for the most part overtaken by good memories. Don't get caught up in where you are today and think that you won't be happy until you reach some distant or imagined destination. Many people think that when they arrive at a certain point, they will be happy. Most folks think that when they retire or when they have a better studio to work at or when they take a trip or reach some financial goal, that they will then be happy. Being goal-oriented is great and must be part of your mission. But don't forget to enjoy the journey as much as the arrival. I imagine your happiest moments will happen along the way, not at the end of the trip. Don't fall into the "**if only**" trap. You can put any goal or dream after that phrase. If you are not careful it can pull you down because you are always looking for something out in the future. Instead of telling yourself "**if only**" make the most of what you have right now, today! No one thing can make you happy or miserable. Take responsibility for your own personal happiness, and don't let anyone or anything steal your joy!

Now it's Your Turn—To Make Your Move!

In each chapter of this book you are encouraged to take action steps to advance. Do not dismiss these actions or put them off. Your decision to reach each point will help you build the right mindset and attitude to attain your full potential. How you think really is a BIG factor on how you will advance. Don't push that aside as pie-in-the-sky thinking. Make it your life plan. Aside from the great achievements you will gain from this thought process, life will be a lot more fun. It should be and needs to be fun as you continue on your journey toward your perfect career! If it is not where you want it to be right at this moment, do not despair. You can change it, fix it or turn it around. You have the tools now. You have always had the tools, but now you have a better understanding of how to use them. It's all in your hands! You can do it if you believe you can.

The entire purpose of this book is to get you to move—from where you are now to where you want to go. You have read this far through the book. So now the question is, what are you going to do about it? Action is the number one key to your progress. To dream, live and then do are the real-life methods that will keep you in a great place mentally, physically and spiritually. Using the tips, strategies and principles in this book will help you in your exciting journey.

Keep in mind: No road is straight all the way through. There are twist and turns, stops and starts, delays, accidents and construction. Your career and your life will be very similar. Expect this to occur along the way. Each hurdle you clear and each step you take to move forward will increase your energy, your empowerment and your focus. Don't stop, don't ever stop! Your breakthrough may be just around the corner. Keep on the lookout for opportunities, and they will find you.

Make A Promise To Yourself Starting Today:

- To be so strong that nothing can disturb your peace of mind.
- Spend time with great people.
- To talk health, happiness and prosperity to every person you meet.
- To make all your friends feel that there is something important in them.
- To smile often and make your optimism come true.
- To think only of the best and to expect only the best.
- To be just as enthusiastic about the success of others as you are about your own.
- Attend great events, seminars and conferences that will prompt you to learn, grow and embrace change.
- Forget mistakes of the past and press on to the greater achievements of the future.
- To give so much time to the improvement of yourself that you have no time to criticize others.
- To decide to make this your best year ever.
- To have fun and laugh often.

Here's to you—I wish that all your dreams, goals and aspirations come to life!

Bravo! Act One Curtain Calls

Remember these things:

- A can-do attitude will take you places
- Your attitude determines your actions or inactions. Your outlook will determine your life's outcome more than any other single factor!
- Choose whom you associate with very carefully and avoid the naysayers at all costs
- You are not what you think you are. What you think, you are
- If you want to change your career or your life, change your vision
- Be sure to create a Life Plan and be all that you can be!
- To evolve and to advance in all you do you must continue to stretch
- Never stop learning, growing and advancing, and you will never burnout
- Don't ever let failure become final
- Your journey is your life
- You have always had the tools, but now you have a better understanding of how to use them. It's all in your hands! You can do it if you believe you can
- Your breakthrough may be just around the corner. Keep on the lookout for opportunities, and they will find you
- Decide to make this your best year ever

Encore! Encore!—Act Two: **Robert Landau**

"Take the first step in faith. You don't have to see the whole staircase, just take the first step." —Martin Luther King, Jr.

Do You Know Denise?

Looking in from the outside, Denise had it all. Seldom had anyone in the dance-teacher world been so lucky. Her rapid rise to fame and fortune had rarely been accomplished by others, and needless to say, she was the envy of her peers. In fact, many of her peers tended to look down on Denise only because it appeared that she had everything handed to her without much effort in return. From the moment she could walk her mother insisted she set her sights on the world of dance. Denise found herself enrolled in a bevy of dance classes—way before she would even know what it is to make a decision for herself. Jazz, tap, ballet, modern, you name it, she mastered it. While other kids her age were playing with their friends after school, Denise never knew what a play date was because she was always in class. Some teachers she loved; others she hated. Denise's Mom loved them all because she knew that her young daughter was getting an education in dance and in life. It really looked as if she was well on track to become a celebrated dance teacher—if that's what she wanted to do with her life.

As is so often the case when a child is told to pursue a path early in life, Denise began to rebel. It got so bad in her later years that her mother had to keep constant track of Denise's attendance issues. Cigarettes, booze and boyfriends moved to the top of her daughter's list, instead of anything having to do with dance. Did Denise win competitions? Oh yes, in quantities too numerous to mention. Did she care? Absolutely not! Hanging out at the mall proved to be far more interesting than the possibility of winning yet another prize at an upcoming competition!

When it came time to graduate from college, Denise found herself in a quandary: "I guess this is what happens when I don't decide on a specific major and take more generalized classes just to get this whole thing over with! So, now what do I do?" Denise had just been given her college diploma as her Dean shook her hand at her graduation ceremony and wished her good luck in the world. "Good luck in the world? What the heck do I do with that?" Denise had no idea what her next move would be. She knew she needed to put bread on her table. One meal a day was making her look rather gaunt. Support from her parents? No way. She had burned that bridge a long time ago.

The next few months were painful reminders on what it feels like to be totally lost and alone in the world. The world was now all too real and raw without the buffer of being in college. "I guess a degree in literature and communications might not have been the best way to go for me after all," she would often admit to herself. It was way too late to do anything about that now. What was she going to do? Sadly, she had absolutely no idea. What would you do if you were Denise?

Denise had finally mustered up enough courage to go to the mailbox. She hadn't been for weeks. Prior to that her mailman started bringing her mail to her apartment door only because the mailbox was overstuffed with all of the mail Denise had been avoiding for weeks. Bills, termination notices—she just didn't want to deal with any of it. "Who cares if I'm out on the street? I'll deal with it if I absolutely have to!" Well, the day finally arrived where she absolutely had to.

Just returning to her apartment from getting a dry, cardboard-tasting hot dog from the corner convenience store, Denise stopped dead in front of her apartment door. Looking right back at her was the manager of the apartment community that Denise called home.

Manager: Hello Denise

Denise: Well hello, Alexis. How are you?

Manager: I'm fine

Denise: What brings you here?

Manager: Denise, I'm here to tell you not one, but two things, both of which I hate having to do. Believe me when I tell you that this is the worst part of my job.

Denise: OK. Go ahead, I guess.

Manager: The animal shelter came by today, and I had to let them into your apartment. They were concerned about reports that your dog wasn't being fed often. Their worst fears were realized when they saw what condition Napoleon was really in. I hate to say it, but they took him back. They've tried calling you, but your phone appears to be out of service. Sorry, Denise. I loved Napoleon. Everyone in the leasing office did.

Denise was stunned. She didn't know what to say.

Manager: I wish I could stop with that, but there's more, Denise. This envelope in my hands is an eviction notice. Please note the date that you'll need to be out of your apartment. It's been quite some time since you've paid your rent, and we just couldn't let that pass anymore. I'm so sorry, Denise. Please let me know if there's anything I can do for you.

And with that, Alexis was gone. Denise just stood there, stunned, hurt and in deep despair. Rather than go into her apartment, she burst into tears and fell into a ball of sobs at her apartment door.

"Oh my God, oh my God, what do I do now?"

It seemed as if Denise was there for hours. She didn't know how long it was, actually. All she knew now was that it was freezing, and she had to go inside just to try to get warm again. Sleep never came to her that night. Now she knew what her friends kept referring to as a "Dark Night of the Soul." Denise lay in her bed on her back; eyes wide open with tears streaming down her face. All kinds of thoughts were running through her mind, for hours on end. "Do I just end it all right now, or do I figure out some way to get myself out of this nightmare?" she kept repeating to herself, over and over, as if it were a mantra. The whole thing was exhausting, to say the least. All she wanted to do was scream to make it all go away.

Not even knowing if she was awake or asleep, at about 4 a.m. that morning, something strange began to happen. Denise felt as if she wasn't alone. Not being totally awake, she wasn't sure if someone had broken into her apartment or if she was just hysterically imagining the whole thing. At one point, she could have sworn she heard someone call her name.

Voice: Denise? . . . Denise?

Denise: Who is there?

Voice: Denise?

Denise: Who is there?

Voice: Listen to me. Can you hear me?

Denise: Who is this?

Voice: Do it.

Denise: What?

Voice: Do it.

Denise: Leave me alone. GO AWAY!

Voice: Do it.

Denise: Do WHAT?

Voice: Denise, you know what to do. Your passion . . . your heartbeat . . . your calling . . . more to do . . . just do it . . . more to do . . . no more time to waste . . . just do it . . . Katherine . . . bye.

Denise: What? What the heck was that! Hello? Is anyone there? If this is a joke, it isn't funny!

Denise wasn't sure what was going on. Had she truly heard it? She didn't think so. At this point she thought her imagination was getting the best of her, and it probably would be best to turn over and finally get some much needed sleep.

Sleep finally came to her, and when she woke up the next morning, Denise was more than grateful. As she lifted herself out of bed, she wondered why her face wasn't dripping from the sloppy kisses her dog, Napoleon, would usually wake her with at this point in time. "Oh my God. I've GOT to get my dog back. Not only that, I've got to get my LIFE back—NOW!"

"OK, OK, so what do I do? Where do I start, what do I do first and even more important, how do I know what to do?" These were all questions that kept plaguing Denise as she stared at the disheveled figure looking back at her in the mirror as she was brushing her teeth.

Just then, she heard it again.

"Denise, you know what to do. Your passion . . . your heartbeat . . . your calling . . . more to do . . . just do it . . . more to do . . . no more time to waste . . . just do it."

Denise didn't know why she was hearing what she heard, but hearing it again brought back distant and vague memories of hearing those words for the very first time just last night. "That's it—I got it!" In a flash, it came to her. "I need to get back into dance, and I need to do it NOW!" All at once Denise's heart began to beat faster—as if she were alive again. She could have sworn she even felt a smile wash over her face as she heard those words for a third time: "Denise, you know what to do. Your passion . . . your heartbeat . . . your calling . . . more to do . . . just do it . . . more to do . . . no more time to waste . . . just do it."

"OK, OK," Denise said. "How do I make getting back into dance happen? Do I just do it?" She knew the answer was a resounding yes. So now Denise was faced with a huge dilemma. How would she get back into something she left so many years ago? She knew that thinking about it was one thing, but actually doing it was another.

"All I can do is just put one foot in front of the other and keep going forward. I was given everything I needed to succeed back in the day. I had all the tools at my disposal to make the success I enjoyed. If I did it then, I can do it now. The choice is mine. I have all the information I need to turn my life around and be the success I was always meant to be. No one is going to do it for me. It's my turn now, as it always was. I had forgotten that most important fact all these years. All I need to do is think how many people don't have all the tools they require to make their lives successful. I was given those tools a long time ago, and I've been sitting on them ever since!"

So here's my question for you: after having read this book up until this point, you have been given so many tools to create true change and success in your profession career. In many ways, you are standing exactly where Denise was standing. How so? After filling yourself with the information we shared in the previous chapters, the choice is now yours to take that information and turn it into action. That's the only way you will take things to the next level in your career as a teacher. Will you be like Denise was in the past, and sit on the knowledge and tools you now have? Or will you take those tools and that knowledge and work hard to turn them into something you can truly be proud of—in your not-too-distant future? It's really up to you.

So how do you take thoughts on paper and turn them into real and tangible results? Don't hit me, but I would answer this question by saying that you just have to do it. Nothing more, but certainly nothing less. What I would also suggest in this case is to take the top five things that you learned in this book that you feel will create a positive change in your role as a teacher, and then create a time-line on paper, mapping out exactly how you will reach the finish line in each of the five areas you've chosen.

So let's say one of the five items happens to be assuming the role as leader. In so doing, you will take more risks in your teaching style. This in turn will go a long way in giving your students a newfound drive and motivation to succeed. Your inspiration will be a spark of motivation for them. In return, your classes will have more of an artistic edge and really stand out when it comes to other teachers' offerings at your studio. This will also go a long way in making your studio stand out among all the others in your area of town.

So how will you get there? Make a time-line on a piece of paper concerning this one goal. Pick specific dates in the near future that you will have your new strategy in place. What will this look and feel like when it comes to you teaching specific classes? Always remember that it's the destination in this case, as well as the journey. Make getting there a series of gradual steps. Do this three weeks from now, four more weeks after that and so on. Then choose a finish-line date when you plan to have everything fully in place on a physical level. This way, you have specific dates —in reality, deadlines—that force you to get things going. This bridges the gap between saying you'll get something into place and actually putting it in place. Words are mere words until they are turned into tangible action.

The biggest downfall people face when they want to achieve goals is that those all too often are unattainable. Even if the goals are achievable, not enough time is given to realize them. People lose interest and become lazy. By putting easy-to-attain goals on paper in the form of days and deadline dates, they get done! What's the point of having the tools you need to succeed, and then putting this book down and never using any of the advice you've been given? Steve, Angie and I can't be there with you to see that you realize your goals. Just as it was for Denise, whether you fail or succeed is totally up to you. Realize that it's your turn. The baton is in your hands. Will you step up and conduct the orchestra to the absolute best of your know-how and abilities? Do it. Just do it. You'll never know if you've failed or succeeded unless you do it. Mean what you say and say what you mean. You are the one who is in control. What if you should fail? No problem. Just get up off the floor, dust yourself off and do it again. You have an even better chance of succeeding because you've done it once before. When something goes wrong during a performance, does everything stop and close down? Do the dancers just leave the stage and the audience goes home? No! The issue occurred but the performance continues. In the grand scheme of things, it's the performance that matters, not the one mistake that occurred during it.

That's exactly what Denise did. Just in case you might be wondering where Denise is today, she's doing absolutely great, thank you very much! She's the owner of not one, not two, but four dance studios in her state, and absolutely loves every minute of it. She makes it a point to let everyone and anyone she knows that they have the power and will to succeed. All they have to do is do it. Not too long ago, Denise called me, and she was even more overjoyed than she usually is. I asked her what she was so jubilant about. She told me that just a couple of days before this, she had figured out something that had remained a mystery to her. When I asked her to share what she was talking about, this is what she told me:

"Just last week I was lying in bed with my dear dog, Napoleon, whom I got back from the shelter. I was so very thankful for so much of what I've seen happen in my life as of late, and then it hit me and hit me hard. Those words that I thought I had heard on my deep, dark night of the soul years ago came flooding back into my conscious. I heard them again just like I did so vividly that night: 'Denise, you know what to do. Your passion . . . your heartbeat . . . your calling . . . more to do . . . just do it . . . more to do . . . no more time to waste . . . just do it . . . Katherine . . . bye.' All these years I was leaving out something very important about that group of words."

Robert: What was that Denise?

Denise: One of the last words of that phrase.

Robert: Do you mean 'just do it'?

Denise: No. But that was very important as well. I'm talking about the name 'Katherine.'

Robert: Katherine?

Denise: Yes. It's strange but when those words were first said to me that night, I really felt as if someone was right there saying them to me. The feeling was this wonderful extreme wave of warmth, loving and caring. Robert, I now know who Katherine was.

Robert: Who was she?

Denise: Katherine had died four years before that night. She spoke them to me that night Robert. I know in my heart of hearts that it was her.

Robert: That's amazing, Denise. But who was Katherine?

Denise: My very first dance teacher who was like a second mother to me. She was the one who encouraged me to make something of myself. All those years, she watched over me as if she could see something in me that I never ever knew I had myself.

Robert: What did she see in you Denise?

Denise: She knew that it was my turn. She could see even back then that I had the tools I needed deep within to make a success out of my life. All I had to do was—

Robert: —Just do it?

Denise: Yes Robert. To just do it.

And so, Denise did. How about you?

Bravo! Act Two Curtain Calls

Remember these things:

- It is your choice and decision to use the many tools you have been given, and turn them into real and tangible results
- How do you do that? You just do it!
- Make sure your goals are reasonable and attainable
- Giving yourself enough time to get there is extremely important
- Whether you fail or succeed is totally up to you. You are the one who is in control
- What if you should fail? Just get up off the floor, dust yourself off and do it again
- You have the power and will to succeed

Encore! Encore!—Act Three: **Angela D'Valda Sirico**

> Real success is finding your lifework in the work that you love.
>
> —*David McCullough*

To dream is a wonderful thing to do, as it sustains us in all that we do. It furthers our progress and success in all aspects of our lives. I do believe that, without dreams, we either stay at one level forever, or slowly wither and die from the lack of excitement and happiness in our daily existence. We all have the power to change and keep fueling our dreams and goals. But like most things in life, these changes and adjustments do not come without the hard work and commitment to make them work. By now you have read the previous chapters and been introduced to three different ways to look at goal-setting. Hopefully you have identified for yourself the ways that you think will work best for you and your dreams. Something to keep in mind is that everything is always in a constant state of change. The people who become successful in pursuing their goals and dreams are the ones who understand the necessity of being flexible and being unafraid of change. To some people, change is interpreted as a negative. It is not unusual for people to be completely terrified of making changes to what may be a reasonably comfortable existence. But just as it is in dance, it is those who push through that barrier of fear or pain who make it to the finish line—in first place. Change is not comfortable, but oh, how rewarding it can be when you know that you pushed past all the barriers created to stop you and emerged triumphant. It gives you the same charge of adrenaline that performers feel when they get that burst of applause and the standing ovation after a great performance.

"Promise me you'll be braver than you believe, and stronger than you seem, and smarter than you think."—Christopher Robin to Pooh

Dance training teaches us to get out in front of an audience and make it believe the story we are telling. It involves having courage and enough confidence and belief in ourselves to carry it off. It also involves creating an illusion. Whether you are a performer or teacher or both, the fact is that once you decide to move on to a more rewarding level, it is completely in your hands to pursue your dreams, set your goals and then activate your plans. When you apply for a new credit card, it is exciting when you have that new card in your hand with the high credit limit. But until you actually activate the card, it doesn't do you a bit of good. It is useless to you. Once activated, then it is up to you to buy wisely and pay your bills on time. There is a responsibility involved. When you set your goals, the responsibility lies with you to take the right action to activate and open the doors so that you can step right through to a new world. You alone can take those steps. But with the help of your friends and family, you will find the courage to stay focused and to battle through when necessary and reach your desired goal for your career and personal life.

So how do you handle it when you are not achieving the goals you have set for yourself? A common reaction is to immediately start doubting yourself and the direction that you are taking. Confucius, one of the world's greatest thinkers, has said, ***"When it is obvious that the goals cannot be reached, don't adjust the goals, adjust the action steps."*** These are terrific words of advice, because once you know what your goals are, you just have to find and take the right avenues to reach them. Most roads do not take a completely straight line—there are twists and turns along the way—and a good driver will carefully navigate to get to the destination. Sometimes those hairpin turns can scare you. Just when you think the road is easy and straight again, you turn the corner and there is a steep drop that takes your breath away and makes the hair stand up on the back of your neck. This is all part of life's journey, and that is exactly how you need to view it not just as the destination you are aiming for. We spend our entire lives on a journey, but if we are always putting off or waiting for the end result, how poor and miserable our daily lives will be. The interesting part about the journey is where you go, who you go with and what you make of each stop along the way.

"Learn from the past, set vivid, detailed goals for the future, and live in the only moment of time over which you have any control: now." —Dennis Waitley

Every time that you take a step forward, do it with the knowledge that failure is always a possibility. Failure really is the best way to learn and progress, because if you never aim high enough or encounter failure, you will always stay on the same level. Yes it does take courage, and yes it does mean going ahead with plans—despite other people's warnings of disaster!! I can't tell you the number of times in my life that I have been told that something I wanted to do couldn't possibly work. Trust me; it has happened so many times that I almost don't believe I will be successful unless someone lets me know it's going to be a disaster! It's kind of that reverse psychology! Dare to step out of that comfort zone and surround yourself with as many forward-thinking people you can find to help you make your dreams a reality?

> "You're never given a wish without also being given the power to make it true. You may have to work for it, however."
> —*Richard Bach*

Making Your Plan

There are a few components necessary for a teacher's plan:

1) Personal growth
2) Professional growth
3) Balance personally
4) Balance professionally
5) Rewards

Personal Growth

Most dance teachers lead pretty hectic lives. Between preparing for classes, semesters, concerts, competitions and traveling to and from work, there isn't usually an awful lot of personal time left over. It is important to sit down and make a note of all the goals that you want to attain in your private life. Perhaps it is to find a boyfriend/girlfriend or significant other who can help you just by being around—and who can also help you to survive. This may just be emotional help or it could be financial assistance—perhaps off-setting some of your expenses. Because our hours are not generally nine to five, it can take a special individual to understand the craziness and ties of a dance teacher's life! Maybe you are perfectly happy on your own with some good friends around you. What's important is that you understand the direction that you would like to go in.

Have you ever thought to yourself, "I would really like to try______?" It could be just something to attempt to make your life better and more rewarding. Maybe it is a personal trainer, losing weight, volunteering for a worthwhile cause, getting involved with your local religious organization—anything that you feel would help you grow as an individual. You don't have much free time, but making room for even one activity that brings you happiness will definitely be worth it.

Professional Growth

There is no time like the present to get started with your plan for professional growth. If you wait for the right time, it may never arrive and you will remain stagnant professionally as long as you work. We human beings have really perfected the art of procrastination, and only we have the power to change that. It simply takes the courage and determination to make some good decisions. In this day and age, it is imperative to learn and grow professionally, and it is by doing this that we empower ourselves to be the best that we can be and give the highest value of training to our students. It also makes us invaluable to any employer, which in turn rewards us financially and in reputation. The first step, as always is to make a plan. If you only teach one style of dance, start to investigate every avenue available to you to learn more about that subject. The truth is we have so much available to us nowadays with computers. But it is also important to enroll in teacher training programs. I cannot overstate the importance of certification for professional credibility. It is also important to network with other teachers because we can learn so much from each other. Google all the available options, and then make a move and while you are at it why not make it part of a vacation also?

Personal Balance

It is so easy to lead an unbalanced life personally. You know what I mean—when your entire existence is tied up with teaching and what is happening at the studio or school where you work. It can be all-enveloping if you permit it to be. To lead a well-balanced and happy life, it's as important to plan those moments into your daily life as you would your work schedule. Perhaps it is even more important, because if you are not reasonably at peace with yourself, you won't give your students and your employer your greatest gifts—which are your knowledge, wisdom and humor. All three of these things are crucial if you are to make the kind of impact that you no doubt would like to make. Take the time to plan fun outings with people you love, time for yourself when you can recharge, and vacation time so that you can step out of the everyday picture and get a new perspective on everything that is happening in your life. Without these moments we just glide through life in a sort of zombie way that does no one, least of all ourselves, any good!

Professional Balance

A semester or a year can go by in a flash, and suddenly you realize you got through it but did very little with it because everything was just so frantic. Good planning is the key to obtaining a really well-balanced professional life.

Of course a plan by itself does not equate to a balanced existence. Without a great action plan attached to it, those good intentions may never be realized. What it really takes is a certain amount of self-discipline and routine to make sure that you achieve your goals in a way that will bring harmony and happiness to your life. This is also a moment when your coping skills are really going to come into play. How do you react when an obstacle to your plans looms up before you? Do you get angry, do you evade the issue and run away or do you face each crisis, both mini and major, with courage and determination to let nothing stand in the way of continuing your plan? Make no mistake, days may go by when everything runs smoothly and life is good, and then—wham! Something unexpected hits you in the face, and there may be a problem. The way that you train yourself to react to these unforeseen circumstances is going to be very important to you and to your well-being. As Henry David Thoreau once said, ***"What you get by achieving your goals is not as important as what you become by achieving your goals."*** This is something to always keep in mind as again, it is all part of the journey and no single incident will determine who you are professionally or what you are capable of.

Structure is important if you are going to progress. If you just meander through you will never get where you want to be. You will have a bunch of regrets and irritation at yourself for not being better organized and willing to take that step forward—even on the days when you least feel like it. We teach our students to have self-discipline and to have good coping skills. Let's not forget that actions speak louder than words, and make sure that we are truly practicing what we preach.

Rewards

What kind of rewards are we talking about? Are rewards necessary? I think that it is important to reward ourselves and to be rewarded by others in some way for every step that we take closer to accomplishing our goals.

Rewards can also be used as an incentive for ourselves, a little treat if you will, for moving unwaveringly toward the finish line.

Rewards can come in different forms and can also be given to you by others. If your employer is happy with the progress you are making with students, he or she may very well reward you with recognition and a raise. You may feel well-rewarded when you see that your choreography does well or that one student who just has not been getting it in your classes suddenly does a complete turnaround. You know, finally, your information has helped him or her to become a much better dancer. You should also set rewards for yourself—perhaps a day devoted just to you with a visit to a spa, a great lunch or dinner with your loved one, or a good friend with tickets to a show that you have been dying to see. It really doesn't matter what kind of reward it is because everyone has his or her own idea of what a blissful time is. Decide to go on that vacation or a weekend getaway, because these moments will renew you mentally and physically and help you to take that next step forward.

> "Success is not final, failure is not fatal: It is the courage to continue that counts."
>
> —*Winston Churchill*

Finding the courage to keep pursuing your goals is not always easy. But as long as you make your plans and put them into action, you will succeed beyond your dreams.

Bravo! Act Three Curtain Calls

Remember these things:

- Without dreams we either stay at one level forever, or slowly wither and die from the lack of excitement and happiness in our day-to-day existence
- People who become successful in pursuing their goals and dreams are the ones who understand the necessity of being flexible and being unafraid of change
- Those who push through the barrier of fear or pain make it to the finish line
- When you set your goals the responsibility lies with you to take the right action to activate and open the doors so that you can step right through to a new world
- Most roads in life do not take a completely straight line. There are twists and turns along the way, and a good driver will carefully navigate to get to the destination
- We spend our entire lives on a journey, but if we are always putting off or waiting for the end result, how miserable our daily lives will be
- The interesting part about the journey is where you go, who you go with and what you make of each stop along the way
- Failure is one of the best ways to learn and progress
- Step out of your comfort zone and surround yourself with as many forward-thinking people you can find to help you make your dreams a reality
- We human beings have really perfected the art of procrastination, and only we ourselves have the power to change that

- The way you react to unforeseen circumstances is very important to you and your well-being
- Always remember to reward yourself for a job well done
- Pursuing your goals is not always easy. But as long as you make your plans and put them into action you will succeed beyond your dreams

NOTES

Chapter 9

Post-Performance Notes

Afterword

Rave Reviews!

Congratulations! You made the journey with us, and we certainly hope it was as wonderful going through all of the informative twists and turns with us as it was for us to take this journey with you. Thank you for walking down this road with us. We couldn't have done it without you. We don't want things to stop here. We need to stick together as time progresses—so we don't view this as the journey's end by any means. We consider you to be a part of our ongoing creative and artistic team. So with that in mind, we invite you to interact with us whenever you might feel moved to do so. Let us know your opinions of what you've just read. Give us suggestions for future books. Ask us any questions you still might have. In other words, the promise we made at the start of our journey will always remain: We are here for you whenever you might need us. All you have to do is connect with us. We'd love to hear from you, so don't be a stranger. Here's how you can connect with us:

Steve Sirico: Steve@danceteacherweb.com
Angela D'Valda Sirico: Angela@danceteacherweb.com
Robert Landau: rl@robertlandaumotivation.com

Here Are Some Great Resources for Products & Services

ACCESS BROADWAY

3137 Lincoln Ave.
Oceanside, NY 11572
(516) 594 - 6050
(516) 594 - 6051 Fax
www.accessbroadway.com
accessbway@aol.com

Access Broadway is the very first "all inclusive" talent competition and convention, featuring dance, acting and voice. Our diverse competition and "Broadway Experience" workshops are judged and taught by an "All Star" faculty with numerous students being placed in Broadway Shows. Our spectacular Las Vegas & Broadway Cup awards are won each year by the nation's top two schools.

ART STONE/THE COMPETITOR

1795 Express Drive North
Smithtown, NY 11788
(631) 582-9500 • (631) 582-9541 Fax
www.artstonecostumes.com
customerservice@artstonecostumes.com

Art Stone/The Competitor ® was the first costume company to use crystal rhinestones, finer velvets, brighter colors and exquisite new fabrics, which gave the dance teacher the opportunity to order professional looking costumes at dancing school prices. We have the lowest prices in the industry, the highest quality, and the most fashion-forward designs. In addition, this year, we have doubled our production so that costumes can be delivered on an "on-time schedule," and customer service has been streamlined so each teacher can have a "personal customer service representative."

ASAMI DESIGNS

Asami Green
(203) 249-0048
www.asamidesigns.com
ag@asamidesigns.com

An experienced graphic designer with diversified design skills in print, branding, marketing, web design, and traditional illustrations and painting.

CAPEZIO

1 Campus Road • Totowa, NJ 07512
(800) 533 - 1887 • (800) 522 - 1222 Fax
www.capezio.com

With over 120 years of world-famous design, performance and comfort behind every step, Capezio® has evolved past the historic beginnings of Salvatore Capezio's corner cobbler shop. Dance has never had a better partner than Capezio®, including the grace of Harmonie and the quality and functionality of Bunheads, Capezio Brands offer bodywear, footwear, legwear and accessories for every dance form, dancer and teacher, including you.

COSTUME GALLERY

4451 Route 130 S. Burlington,
NJ 08016
386 - 6601 • (609) 386 - 0677 Fax
www.costumegallery.net
Kaylee@costumegallery.net

See the Costume Gallery Difference...Exclusive Money Back Dazzle Guarantee; every call answered LIVE by an experienced Customer Service Representative - no waiting; over 360 brand new styles; video of every style at www.costumegallery.net; no bare midriffs. With Costume Gallery you're not just buying costumes, you're buying peace of mind.

CURTAIN CALL

333 East 7th Avenue
York, PA 17404
(888) 808 - 0801
(800) 839 - 1039 Fax
www.curtaincallcostumes.com
curtaincall@performgroupllc.com

Curtain Call Costumes - classic and character costumes for ballet, jazz, tap and performance wear including dance dresses. Curtain Call is the largest designer and manufacturer of dance recital costumes in the world, serving dance schools, civic ballet companies, high schools, colleges and dance teams.

DANCE TEACHER WEB

1580 Post Road
Fairfield, CT 06824
(203) 545 - 7167
(203) 256 - 8910 Fax
www.danceteacherweb.com
danceteacherweb@aol.com

Dance Teacher Web was founded in 2007 by Steve Sirico and Angela D'Valda Sirico to give dance teachers and studio owners the tips, tools and tactics to gain, train and retain better students. The online service offers members new choreography in all dance disciplines on a monthly basis, plus features on marketing dance businesses and running all back office operations. The presenting faculty on D.T.W. are respected professionals with a wealth of knowledge and a passion to share their expertise with you. The number one goal is to help give ongoing support and to create a place for teachers to re-energize and refresh 24 hours a day! The sharing of ideas, knowledge and success is what it is all about. Every year Dance Teacher Web produces a conference and expo where DTW comes to life. Join us at the Creative Oasis!

DANCE - IN A BOX

1951 W. Carson Street
Torrance, CA 90501
(310) 755 - 4973
(310) 320 - 4381 Fax
www.danceinabox.com
tricia@danceinabox.com

Hip Hop made easy! Dance - In a Box is your online source for choreography, music and dance related activities. Create hip hop routines for ages 3-adults in 3 easy steps with our interactive choreography kits! Plus, download routines, music and more! Visit www.danceinabox.com to make teaching hip hop EASY!

DANCE INFORMA www.DanceInforma.com

Dance Informa is the industry's leading online dance publication for teachers, professionals and students of all dance styles. Dance Informa publishes informative articles and is a great resource for teachers and their students. Latest Dance News / Dance Shows and Events in your region Nationwide Audition Listings / Interviews with industry leaders Reviews of current dance works and festivals Advice, tips and resources / Health advice / Giveaways Directories - including a Teachers and Choreographers Directory!

DANCE TEACHER SUMMIT

Katy Malone
(212) 586-7000
info@danceteachersummit.com
www.danceteachersummit.com

The Dance Teacher Summit was created to bring together like-minded dance teachers who have a passion for the growth and development of dance education. The event is specifically designed for and attended by studio owners, studio teachers, K-12 educators, dance professors and teaching assistants from across the globe. The world renowned faculty for this unique event will combine the expertise of legendary master teachers with the cutting edge styles of today's most influential choreographers. This 3-day conference, held in New York City, includes dance classes, business and marketing seminars, interactive panel discussions, guest performances, a fashion show, the industry's leading vendors and more! The Dance Teacher Summit promises to give dance teachers the motivation and inspiration they need to re-energize their passion for the art and the business of teaching dance.

DOUBLE PLATINUM / THEATRICALS DANCE FOOTWEAR BY DISCOUNT DANCE SUPPLY

5065 E.Hunter Avenue
Anaheim, CA 92807
(714) 970 - 0462
(714) 970 - 9075 Fax

Double Platinum Performancewear is fresh, exciting and in stock. We now offer a large selection of children's costumes. Make extra profits at your studio with Theatricals Dance Footwear. Theatricals high quality and the lowest priced footwear in the industry. Both brands brought to you by the name you trust: Discount Dance Supply.

EN POINTE ENTERPRISES

Linda Gillam • 866-491-9019
www.en-pointe.com
www.facebook.com/danceproducts
www.twitter.com/danceproducts

En Pointe is a manufacturer of dance barres, and sprung flooring and a distributor for glassless mirrors, 'marley' dance floor surfaces and staging. En Pointe has been supplying dance equipment across North America and the world for over fifteen years. Quality products designed by dancers for dancers.

FINANCIAL GROOVE

10040 Bonterra Avenue
Las Vegas, NV 89129
(702) 966 - 0127
(702) 966 - 0289 Fax
www.FinancialGroove.com
info@FinancialGroove.com

Financial Groove bridges the gap between creativity and business. We organize, create and facilitate the best bookkeeping, tax services and systems to make small businesses in the arts financially successful. We provide you with the tools and coaching to inspire and achieve success in growing your dance studio.

GTM SPORTSWEAR

520 McCall Road
Manhattan, KS 66502
(785) 410 - 6128
www.gtmsportswear.com
melissa@igtm.com

GTM Sportswear is your 100% customer satisfaction, value driven stop for all of your apparel needs. From practice to performance, we have some of the best selection and great prices. Stop by and check us out today!

INTERNATIONAL DANCE SUPPLIES

Harlequin House
Forde Court
Newton Abbot
Devon TQ14 4BT
(866) 939 - 8909
www.idsdance.com

International Dance Supplies was founded in 1978 in England by Dance Teacher, Anne Walker. The UK's number 1 dancewear supplier launched a range of quality dance accessories in America in 2009. Their reputation growing, in 2010 IDS was awarded the contract for the coveted American Ballet Theatre Training Program Uniform.

JAZZ TAP CENTER - THE MILLER & BEN TAP SHOES

P.O. Box 821
New York, NY 10108
(646) 383 - 4949
www.JazzTapCenter.com
Tap@JazzTapCenter.com

Home of Avi Miller, Ofer Ben, Tap Tel-Aviv Dance Troupe and The Miller & Ben Tap Shoes - one of the world's best 'Musical Tap Instruments', elegant, comfortable, hand-made shoes, in nine models and 50 colors and patterns. The JTC is also the production office for the Tradition In Tap Workshops in New York City.

JUMP DANCE CONVENTION

Gil Stroming
(212) 397-3600
info@breakthefloor.com
www.breakthefloor.com

Jump is the largest dance convention in the world, touring to 22 US cities and 7 international cities. Each event includes a top-rate workshop, with more class time offered per city than any other convention in the industry. Jump also offers a first-class competition with fair, credible judging in a fun and supportive environment. Jump is something that's high energy, fresh and innovative. It is a change from the assembly line of dance competitions and conventions across America. Most importantly, it's an inspiring, educational event for all levels and ages.

MARQUETTE PRODUCTIONS
M-POWER DANCE WORKSHOPS

(267) 243 - 0442
www.marquetteproductions.com
www.mpowerdance.com

The dancer's source for all of your music editing and creation needs! We'll make sure your dance studio, theater company or dance team is performing with platinum quality music! Our services have been used by professional choreographers Michelle Barber, Lara Luzim, and Jose De La Cuesta! Use the editing service the professionals trust and find out why people are saying Marquette Productions… "will always be my go to editor for music!"

MEMORY MAKERS

1530-119th Street
Whiting, IN 46394
(219) 659 - 2042
www.photosbymemorymakers.com
johnlovasko@gmail.com

Providing Professional Photography for dance schools. Affordable dance photo packages as low as $12! Earn a "Rebate" on photo sales! We provide the complete package from posing to mailing photos to homes. Call for details (219) 659-2042. We consider it a privilege to be your photographer.

MODE DION

P.O. Box 1123
Palm Desert, Ca. 92261
(760) 837-9433
www.modedion.com
cdnm@modedion.com

Mode Dion offers high quality stage make-up and professional products with support and education including books, DVD's, website (beauty training and shopping), "Makeup University" You Tube Channel and Face Book with tips/updates. Make-up kits and bulk discounts available for studio owners.

MOTION POWER BY TIGERSSIX

http://motion.tigersix.com
475 Rosemary Ave Suite 202
West Palm Beach, FL 33401
888-910-8060

MOTION is the result of dance studio owners and teachers working directly with software developers to create a product not currently found on the market today. MOTION will allow studio owners and teachers to spend less time managing the business and more time teaching. MOTION is simple and easy to use. MOTION was designed to for the computer novice. MOTION is a complete solution for the dance studio. MOTION gives a fully functioning website, online shopping, online registration, email and text notifications!

MUSIC EDITING ONLINE.COM

8950 W. Olympic Blvd. #512
Beverly Hills, CA 90211
(310) 597 - 0708
www.musiceditingonline.com
Jack@musiceditingonline.com

MusicEditingOnline.com is a full service music mixing and remixing service for Choreographers, Dance Teachers, Coaches and all multimedia shows and projects.

ROBERT LANDAU MOTIVATION

robertlandaumotivation.com
rl@robertlandaumotivation.com

Robert Landau is an International Motivational Speaker, Seminar Facilitator and a Master of Ceremonies. He is a Positive Results Expert adept at helping businesses and individuals achieve amazing positive results. His website, among other things, offers a wide variety of affordable best-selling self-help products.

ROYAL ACADEMY OF DANCE

1712 19th Street Suite 215-B
Bakersfield, CA 93301
(661) 336 - 0160
(661) 336 - 0162 Fax
www.radusa.org
info@radusa.org

The Royal Academy of Dance is one of the world's largest and most influential dance education, teacher training and membership organizations. With approximately 13,000 members, its influence has spread to 79 countries and is represented by a network of 34 international offices.

REVOLUTION DANCEWEAR

6100 West Howard
Niles, IL 60714
(800) 806 - 1157
(800) 999 - 5348 Fax
www.revolutiondance.com
info@revolutiondance.com

Revolution Dancewear shares your passion for dance. We sell exclusively to dance schools who wish to provide their students with the highest quality shoes, apparel and costumes at affordable prices. We make selling dancewear and recital costumes easy and profitable for studios and believe the instructor is uniquely qualified to decide what products students should wear.

STAGESTEP

4701 Bath Street #46
Philadelphia, PA 19137
(800) 523 - 0960
(267) 672 - 2912 Fax
www.stagestep.com
stagestep@stagestep.com

When it comes to dance floors, Stagestep provides the materials, experience, and expertise to assist you in making an informed choice at a guaranteed low price. Subfloors, wear surfaces, finish, maintenance, and installation materials are in stock ready to ship.
Each customer gets a customized flooring system to meet specific needs. Call for information and a no-obligation quote.

STEP IN TIME

1305 Boardman Canfield Road
Boardman, OH 44512
(800) 837 - 2042
www.stepintimeinc.com
info@stepintimeinc.com

Welcome to Step In Time Inc... the premier site for all your Team, Stage, Street and Cheerleading needs! We specialize in original creative designs to silk-screen, embroider, or crystallize. Experience our line of active wear and get the TOTAL LOOK! Whether you are looking for dance recital t-shirts, competition team jackets, custom dance costumes, or costume garment bags - we have them all.

"This is the one and only conference for teachers. No other can compare."

A. Shoquist, Dance FX

DanceTeacherWeb Live

The Conference & Expo That Gives YOU More!

The Dance Teacher Web LIVE Conference & Expo brings to life everything that is unique about DanceTeacherWeb.com and the DTW Express...four days of interactive sessions designed to provide you with the latest in teaching tools and business strategies. Our roster of presenters features highly respected and often requested master teachers, up and coming choreographers and business leaders. Seminars, demonstrations and hands-on workshops covering a very wide range of topics will send you home with more practical, usable material than ever before!

"BRILLIANT"

"SO MANY NEW IDEAS"

MORE than 90 Classes Available

MORE Master Teachers Eager To Share Their Knowledge

MORE Presenters & Innovative Ideas For Your Business

MORE Value And Luxury For Your Dollar

MORE Special Events, Expo Resources & Prizes

Expect MORE... You Deserve It!

"WHIRLWIND OF AWESOMENESS"

- **Payment Plans**
- **Group Discounts**
- **Earlybird Specials**
- **Attendee Spotlight Become a presenter at LIVE**

DanceTeacherExpo.com

(203) 545-7167